Sunja's story is a lesson on true empow_____ _____, _____ .__.__ of one seemingly powerless woman on her own journey of faith turns out to be the most powerful, convicting tale of a true modern-day evangelist. A real how-to book for every Christian, for every wife and mother, without the lists and steps but with the lived experience of a woman of God who walked through the small and big trials of life. This autobiographical book turns out to be a love story between God and His daughter, more transformative and real than any fairy tale . . . and yet we do see that by the end of the story, an ordinary woman has become a princess, and we realize that we were following along the life story of a daughter of the Most High King.

MAY SONG, former assistant United States attorney

Sunja Kang Choi's memoir *From Death to Life* is a gripping account of a Christian woman's faith journey. This life story is historical and evangelistic at the same time. Chronicling challenging circumstances with biblical and theological references demonstrates how a faithful follower of Jesus can interpret the vicissitudes of life. This thoughtful presentation is an encouragement to believers and seekers whose life circumstances may be quite different—yet equally worth seeing under the sovereign eye of a loving heavenly Father.

DR. STEPHEN KELLOUGH, chaplain emeritus, Wheaton College

Sunja Kang Choi's story will confront you with God's miraculous yet intimate work in a human life. From Korea to the United States, her expansive memoir elucidates the way God works in two countries and over many generations. With a deep commitment to the Gospel and the Word of God, she presents her personal encounter with God's miraculous power and provision. *From Death to Life* should be read slowly and devotionally as an aid to our own deepening in the gospel, Scripture, and the power of our living God.

MATT ERICKSON, Senior Pastor, Eastbrook Church

Mrs. Choi's winsome testimony of her journey with God provides a window into her search and discovery of the reality of God's saving grace, confirmed by the presence of His Holy Spirit. She tells of the Lord's wondrous deeds in faithfully meeting her family members and friends with His healing, compassion, wisdom, and understanding. Through her account, Mrs. Choi offers a loving gift of encouragement to readers who know the Lord as well as an invitation to any who are seeking to discover Him for themselves.

MARILYN BRENNER, Ministry Associate (Retired), Wheaton College

I've had the honor of knowing Mrs. Choi for the past 25 years through my friendship with her son Dave. And though she has physically aged in that time, somehow she has grown younger. She has grown more childlike in her faith, in her joy, in her love for her Abba Father. Her memoir perfectly captures this childlike faith and her intimate love relationship with her Lord. Out of that love relationship, she has lived a life consumed by a desire to share the good news of Jesus Christ with others. As you read this beautiful memoir, you, too, will be inspired to live with such childlike faith, such intimacy, and such passion for Christ.

DANIEL SON, Lead Pastor, COTB Seattle

From Death to Life

A memoir of God's grace
and faithfulness

Sunja Kang Choi

ISBN: 979-8-7625-4879-3
Imprint: Independently Published

DEDICATION

I dedicate this book to God, who is our Creator and speaks through His holy Bible.

Man is destined to die once, and after that to face judgment.

Hebrews 9:27

For every house is built by someone, but God is the builder of everything.

Hebrews 3:4

CONTENTS

ACKNOWLEDGMENTS

In light of this book's publication, I would like to give special thanks to Mrs. Becky Heusner. She has been helping me to edit these writings as a voluntary ESL teacher with the love of Jesus Christ. Without her sacrificial contribution, this book would not have been completed. I also thank everyone who read through the manuscript and gave suggestions. That includes Karen Trichardt, Pastor William Wu, Shelley Germain, Dr. Chip Hardy, and my niece Sujin Kang.

I want to thank Leanne Rolland for offering her incredibly experienced talent of editing. She spent countless hours poring through the manuscript to help improve it and was patient and kind with English being my second language. This book would not be what it is without her. Also, I want to thank Julie Chen, whose wonderful eye for photography produced the beautiful cover of the book.

Lastly, I thank my four beloved sons given to me by God. Each of them helped me so much in writing this book. Sam gave a first reading and offered very helpful suggestions. David took my handwriting and typed the book into the computer. He also did much editing. John helped with a lot of administrative work. Paul served by giving suggestions for the artistic side of the book.

I am so thankful that God provided such a humble team to help with my many weaknesses. As English is my second language, this task would have been impossible without these brothers and sisters. They spent tireless hours helping me improve this book. If there are any shortcomings, those are solely mine. May our Father's grace and favor be with all of your serving hearts to the glory of our King!

FOREWORD

I was only four years old, but I remember it like it was yesterday. I had just woken up and walked out of the cramped bedroom I shared with my older brother. In our family room, we had an old, worn-out coffee table that comfortably seated six people. The bright morning sun hit my eyes, and I squinted to see who was visiting our home. There were about ten women packed around the table eagerly listening as my mom taught them the gospel from the book of John. She taught with a joy and authority that captivated the other women. Week after week, my mom would faithfully teach them the way to know Jesus as their actual Savior. And week after week, another person would put their faith in Jesus. Fast forward four decades and not much has changed, although by grace, I no longer live at home with my mom. However, I still meet many women who have been walking with Jesus all these years because of the gospel witness of my mom. They come to me and hold my hand with gratitude as they tell me how my mom loved them and shared Jesus with them until they, too, were born again. They are the living fruit that affirms what I believe: that I know of no greater personal evangelist than my mom.

For over forty years I have seen her share Christ, both in fluent Korean and sometimes in broken English, with coworkers, church friends, professors, strangers on buses, planes, and in taxi cabs, and with me. Whenever I go on a speaking trip with my mom, I know that whoever the third person in our row is will hear the gospel at some point. On a long flight to Hawaii, a retired doctor sat by us. As the flight departed, my mom began to strike up conversation. When the talk turned to Jesus, the doctor put her newspaper up between her and my mom, a clear sign that she did not want to be bothered with religious talk. My mom silently prayed until the lady's arms got tired from holding the paper up. My mom took that as a sign to continue talking about Jesus. This happened a couple more times. Newspaper goes up. My mom silently prays. Doctor's arms get tired. Mom continues to share the gospel. Needless to say, I was uncomfortable with my mom not receiving the clear social cues. As the conversation continued, however, I noticed the doctor becoming more attentive to my mom's presentation of the gospel. Toward the end of the flight, my mom got up to go to the bathroom. It was then that the retired doctor turned to me, and with a grateful voice said, "Your mom is a really special lady."

On another occasion, we landed at the airport and took a cab to the hotel to meet the rest of our family. I noticed the driver was an older Korean man, so I relayed the information quietly to my mom. As soon as I told her, I knew what was coming next. She spoke to him in Korean with a minute or two of small talk, and then she went in with the gospel. He opened up about how he went to church as a kid but that he no longer attended or believed. As we were coming to the end of our thirty-minute drive, she said to the driver, "Please read the Gospel of John and Romans." He didn't seem interested. A couple of minutes later, she said, "Please consider reading the Gospel of John and Romans." After we arrived at the hotel, I asked my mom, "Why did you repeat that when he seemed disinterested?" She replied, "Because he needs to understand the gospel, and John and Romans present the gospel so clearly. The gospel is the only way he will receive eternal life." I remember being so convicted. If we really believed what my mom believed, wouldn't we all share Christ with such conviction and love?

As amazing as her bold witness is, her faith is expressed most in her daily character. When I try to describe her to friends, I struggle with the words because they can never do justice to the woman of God my mom is. She lives out her faith every day. She loves people that others avoid. If she sees any homeless person, she always stops to tell them about Christ's love and hands them money, even when I interject with my enlightened knowledge of what they will do with her money. When anyone visits my mom's house, they always leave with a full stomach, an encouraged soul, and some gift or food to take home. My mom would come to my church each week with a suitcase filled with snacks for different members and a Christian book or Bible to bless someone who was exploring Christianity. In fact, whenever she met a new believer or seeker, she would write their name down because English is her second language and she didn't want to forget the person. Then she could go home and bring them back something to encourage them the following week. She would often roast peanuts, and church members would boast about receiving the coveted hand-roasted delights. I had to remind them to stay humble.

When I was nineteen years old, I was diagnosed with Hepatitis B and was told by the doctor that the virus could lead to cancer and eventually to death. My mom prayed for me from three a.m. throughout the morning. When I thanked her, she responded, "How much should a parent sacrifice for the sake of their children? And how much more, when my child is sick, should I pray for him? And this is what I prayed for you, Son: 'Father, take away the sickness from my son and put it on me.'" I knew my mom meant every word of it. She would rather suffer through the cancer herself and die so that her son could live a long and healthy life. Later that night, when I was alone in my dorm room, the Lord impressed this thought upon my mind: "Why are you amazed at your mother's love? I did something so much greater. I sent my Son into the world, and He took upon Himself the sickness of the world—sin—so that the world could be eternally healed of their spiritual sickness." Through my mom's sacrificial love, God showed me one of the greatest pictures of the gospel I had ever experienced.

In the weeks after my diagnosis, my mom would drive up to my college and feed me healthy soup and tea she had painstakingly prepared for me every day. I often expressed annoyance that I had to eat such bitter things or said that I was too busy. But she, with the loving heart of a godly mother, continued to bring them so that I would have a chance at health.

I have so many memories of her singing hymns while washing dishes or while driving us to school. So many of the hymns are etched into my heart because of her singing. I recall a time when my mom called me and sounded extremely sad.

It was the saddest I had ever heard her on the phone. I felt my heart sink, and it continued to be heavy throughout the next day. The next night, I called to check in on her, but her voice had brightened since the previous day. Surprised, I asked my mom, "What happened? You sound happier!" She replied, "I read through the book of Jeremiah for several hours this morning, and God lifted me up through His Word." The Bible was the prescription for her gloomy soul.

When my mom was first diagnosed with cancer, I remember how hard our family took it. She has been the steady presence of joy and love in our family for all of our lives. The morning of my mom's surgery, we all went around and prayed with tears that God would heal her. When we finished, my mom sheepishly asked if she could pray too. I remember saying, "Of course, Mom!" She prayed with the most pure and childlike faith. "Father, You have held my hand every day since You saved me. As I go into this surgery, would You hold my hand, and by Your grace, would You hold my hand out of the surgery as well." I was so moved by the intimacy and tenderness with which she prayed. Tears filled my eyes as we all sensed the manifest presence of God in that room. By His grace, she has been cancer free now for over five years.

Recently, I went through a painful season where I fell into a deep depression and was unable to see hope. When I asked if my mom would still love me if I were to leave the ministry, she spoke firmly, "You will always be my son." A couple of weeks later, when I asked her a second time, tears welled up in her eyes as she said, "I would give my life away for you, my son." All of my brothers have their own stories of how my mom has loved them with unconditional love or how, through her life and her words, she has modeled the unshakable conviction that Christ alone is King and Savior and that every person needs to hear the gospel and move from death to life.

I have always wished that everyone could meet my mom. I want every person who is ambivalent or apathetic about Christianity to see my mom's joy in the midst of suffering, her willingness to forgive those who have wounded her so deeply, and her love for those who have yet to turn to God. Now, through this book, a part of that dream comes true. This is just a small portrait of a life lived with great joy under the authority of God's Word and in the fullness of the Holy Spirit.

Pretty much every night before I go to bed, I thank my heavenly Father from the depths of my heart that He gave me a mom who so clearly and obviously shines the light of the glory of Christ. I pray you also will thank God for her testimony after you have read this book. And more importantly, that you will love Jesus the way my mom has for over fifty years.

–David Choi

PREFACE

By the time I finish this book, I will be seventy-seven years old. At this age, I have had much time to reflect on my short life on this earth. So many things that seemed important when I was young are no longer foremost. As we live our lives on the earth, many of us may focus on obtaining what is needed for success in this life. Fame, wealth, pleasure, security, comfort, and health are what people seek as their top priorities. However, in chasing these things, we may be forgetting what is truly important. Our stay on the earth is fleeting, and as our lives come to an end, what we have been chasing after will become just as transient as our time on the earth. As no human being can know the time of their death, we should prepare ourselves not for what this life promises but for what awaits us after death. Therefore, the most important thing we can do in this life is to prepare for eternal life and the ultimate reward that lies beyond. By preparing for eternal life, our current lives will be transformed in incredible ways we humans cannot imagine, changing the way we live our daily lives. It is truly amazing how God blesses the lives of those who live for **eternal life**. In this book, I would like to humbly share my own journey toward eternal life and how I received citizenship in the Kingdom of God, our imperishable home, and have also been blessed with a *spiritually* prosperous and successful life. I sincerely hope this testimony will be a great encouragement and challenge to you. May our awesome Creator's wisdom and blessings be with you forever!

Just as **man is destined to die once**, and **after that to face judgment [of God]**. (Hebrews 9:27)

All men are like grass, and all their glory is like the flowers of the field; the grass withers and the flowers fall. (1 Peter 1:24)

So we fix our eyes not on what is seen, but on what is unseen. For what is seen is temporary, but what is unseen is eternal. (2 Corinthians 4:18)

INTRODUCTION
THE WAY HOME

I came to the United States of America in July of 1974 as the wife of an international student. I spent most of my time at home bringing up four wonderful boys, rarely venturing out of my immediate neighborhood. However, I had always been interested in the lives of the elderly living alone in the States, since I had taken a course on American family relationships during graduate school. Thus, as soon as I had a chance, I got a job where I could help and assist the elderly.

My first assignment as a Certified Nurse Aide (CNA) was to take care of a woman who was ninety-one years old from three o'clock in the afternoon to eleven o'clock at night. Her house was located in a distant town that I had never been to. This made me anxious as I drove to her house, but thanks to God, I arrived at her home safely.

When my work was finished, the nurse for the next shift came, and I asked her if she could share with me a shortcut to get back to my house. This turned out to be a big mistake. As I followed the directions that she gave me, it seemed as if I were in a maze. I realized that I had gotten lost and became worried that I may not be able to find my way back home. It was then that I spotted a man walking on the sidewalk. I stopped the car and asked him for directions. He confidently told me the way I should go, and so I began driving again. But after a while, I realized I was lost again. This was many years ago—before GPS. My fear and anxiety intensified as it was already past midnight. But then I saw a gas station and pulled in to ask the night attendant if he could help me get home. He explained the route, and I was able to follow his directions. After about fifteen minutes, I recognized familiar buildings. My heart overflowed with gratitude, joy, and relief, replacing my feelings of unease and fear.

When I look back on this experience, I am reminded of an important truth about the road of life. When I received the wrong directions, I became lost and was filled with anxiety and fear. However, when I received the right directions, I found joy, peace, and satisfaction. In our lives, when we find these signs, they are like markers to our home, and that fills our hearts with peace, joy, and calm. This is how we know we are heading home.

I believe that there are many people on this earth who also feel lost from time to time. Many of us are not sure where we are going or where we came from. As we seek to know the right way to go, there are times that we become confused by wrong information. Just as I needed to meet a person who could tell me the right directions to get to my earthly home, I needed to meet the right people to show me the way to reach my heavenly home. My testimony is such a story.

Jesus said, "I am the way [to God] and the truth and the [eternal] life. No one comes to the Father except through me." (John 14:6).

In the book of Isaiah, the Scriptures say, "I am the LORD your God, who teaches you what is best for you, who directs you in the way you should go." (Isaiah 48:17)

1
MY PARENTS' CONVERSION

At a young age, my maternal grandfather, who lived in a small rural town in South Korea, traveled to Seoul, the capital, to study English. There he met an American missionary who was sharing the gospel in English. After my grandfather learned from the Bible, he accepted God as the Creator of the universe and received Jesus Christ as the Savior of the world. My grandfather then returned to his hometown, where he started a small church and ceased participating in the traditional ritual of ancestor worship. As a result, he was beaten and persecuted by his own relatives. But despite these painful trials, my grandfather brought my mother up in the Christian faith.

However, when my mother left her hometown to attend a junior high school in a bigger city, she stopped going to church. Upon graduating from high school, she married my father, whose parents' religion was Buddhism. Consequently, my mother became a passionate Buddhist and memorized many pages of Buddha's writings, and she often took me to the Buddhist temple.

As I was growing up, my young father was unexpectedly diagnosed with tuberculosis, which was difficult to cure in those days. As his illness progressed, he was forced to resign from his job and was hospitalized for many months. He was only thirty-six years old. When my father was eventually discharged from the hospital and returned home, he had not recovered from the disease. He could not sleep due to a continuous fever from a serious lung infection, and it continued to worsen. This fever became almost unbearable, and he could hardly sleep.

I remember vividly the day when my father's friend visited and told us, "He will die before long." My mother was filled with immense grief upon hearing this.

In the 1950s, it was almost impossible for those who were housewives to

3

get a job. Our country was impoverished from the ravages of the Korean war that took place from 1950–1953. My father's tuberculosis greatly worsened in 1953, and if my father had passed away, his seven children—including me—would have been sent to orphanages.

Thus, in the hopes of getting my father healed, my mother prayed fervently to Buddha day and night, but she received no answer. One day, filled with despair, my mother was walking along the street. It was then that she heard a familiar hymn and saw a church building nearby. She went inside the church and listened to the sermon. The minister's message on that day touched her heart. The words played in her ears as truth. From that Sunday onward, my mother ceased going to the Buddhist temple and began attending church.

One Sunday morning, when my mother was getting ready to go to the church, my father asked her, "Would you please pray to God for my recovery?" I could not believe that my father requested a prayer for himself because, as an atheist, he used to discourage his children from going to church. After this, my mother decided to go to the early morning prayer service, which began at five o'clock in the morning. My mother prayed for my father every day, and one night my father had a dream. In the dream, an extraordinarily bright light shone on him as he walked along the street. After a while, he reached a big temple that resembled the temple in Jerusalem and heard a magnificent voice saying, "You have now come to God's temple." When he heard that voice, he coughed once and woke up from the dream, but the phlegm continued. My father began to worry that the mucus he was coughing out was full of blood and that he may die soon. Eventually, the coughing began to subside. When he turned the light on, he saw a large amount of dirty mucus, but there was no blood. After that night, my father's terminal lung infection and his severe fever miraculously disappeared.

Through this, our family witnessed a wondrous miracle. The medical doctors had given up on my father. There was no hope at all—until God's supernatural hand appeared. By God's divine power and His amazing grace for our family, my siblings and I were spared from going to an orphanage. How could my father be healed by the almighty Creator? I had pondered over this supernatural healing power that did not involve any surgery or medical treatment by the doctors.

Later, I read in God's Word:

Call to me and I will answer you and tell you great and unsearchable things you do not know. (Jeremiah 33:3)

The LORD is good to those whose hope is in him, to the one who seeks him. (Lamentations 3:25)

God disciplines us for our good, that we may share in his holiness. (Hebrews 12:10)

According to God's words, I believe that God heard my father's urgent request to my mother to pray for his healing, even though he was an atheist. He also heard my mother's numerous, heartbreaking prayers. For this reason, our gracious and merciful God came to cure my father for the sake of our whole family. I believe that God called my parents to Him through this tribulation.

After my father experienced this miracle, he testified, "I was an atheist before, but now I believe there is an almighty God who is beyond my knowledge and understanding in this universe. He has healed me. Therefore, from now on, we will all go to church." At the time, my father was thirty-eight years old.

By God's great grace, my father became an earnest Christian. He continued to trust in God for the rest of his life, and God blessed him abundantly. He became the mayor of the city of Taegu, which is the third largest city in South Korea. Later, he became one of the administrative secretaries in the Blue House, which is Korea's equivalent to the White House in the United States. He passed away at the age of sixty-eight: God had graciously given him thirty more years. In all those years, he always humbled himself before God. My mother told me a touching story about my father. While he was mayor, he always had a big Bible on his desk, and whenever someone came to the office with important requests, my father used to point them to the Bible and tell them that they should ask God first.

I miss my gentle and loving father so much. I often reminisce about him with fond memories. By God's grace, he was transformed and came to faith, to the shepherd of his soul.

Without faith it is impossible to please God, because anyone who comes to him must believe that he exists and that he rewards those who earnestly seek him. (Hebrews 11:6)

You were like sheep going astray, but now you have returned to the Shepherd and Overseer of your souls. (1 Peter 2:25)

2
SEARCHING AFTER GOD

When I was ten years old, my family started to attend a Presbyterian church. I regularly attended Sunday school and was a member of the children's choir. I learned about heaven and hell in Sunday school. The teacher showed us a painting of heaven with all its beauty and hell with an engulfing fire. He said, "If you believe in God and His only Son, Jesus Christ, who died on the cross for our sins, and if you obey God's words in your daily life, you will go to heaven. Otherwise, you will end up in hell."

The teacher continued, "You can cheat on your parents and friends, but you cannot cheat on God because the eyes of the Lord range throughout the earth. He always watches over whatever you do and wherever you go." After I heard this, I tried to correct myself from lying and from other bad behaviors. I wanted to be a righteous person in God's sight, and by doing this, I thought that I believed in God.

When I became a college student, I served in the church as a Sunday school teacher as well as a youth group teacher. I was also a choir member and a leader of the young women's group. Sometimes I cleaned the floors of the church building when they needed it. I thought that this was the way I should live as a Christian who belongs to the church. But as I grew older, my faith often came at odds with my rational mind. Whenever I observed the wondrous order of the universe and the mystery of life, I saw the possibility that there might be an almighty God who is the Maker and Ruler of this universe. However, there were also many doubts, and I could not bring myself to feel confident of God's existence.

I had six basic questions about what is unseen:

1. Where did I come from?
2. Where am I going after death?

3. Are heaven and hell real?
4. What is the purpose of my short life?
5. Is God real?
6. How can I believe in an invisible God?

The last question was the most important to me. If I could believe in God's existence, the other questions would be answered in light of that reality. Therefore, I wanted to seek God, the creator of this world. And I thought that the revival worship service, where pastors perform supernatural signs for the sick and the congregation sought divine signs and visions, would be a good starting point.

When I attended a revival service for the first time, what I observed was a noisy and disorderly environment. At first, I could not bring myself to feel comfortable with the pattern of the service. But as the services continued, I began to see some miracles among them, and I joined in by clapping my hands.

I would pray during the service, "Dear God, I want to know the meaning of this short life, as we have no guarantee for tomorrow. Most of all, I want to perceive Your presence. Would You please give me a sign directly? I think I could believe in Your existence if I experienced one of these things: speaking in divine tongues, having a divine vision, or a miraculous healing of my intestinal troubles that no doctor can cure."

For three years, I wandered from place to place, hoping to experience one of these signs. Throughout this time, I saw other people receiving some of these signs during the services, but I never received any of them for myself, no matter how diligently I searched. After three long years of searching, I said to myself, "There is no God. If there is a God, He would have heard my earnest prayers and answered me." I was deeply discouraged.

It was at that time when one of the most important events in my life took place. I had been going to church for over fifteen years, attending weekly and serving the church religiously. That is why this decision was so important and difficult. But finally, I decided to leave my beloved church because I thought there was no God in the church either.

Three weeks after leaving the church, I was bothered by a mild feeling of guilt and fear, especially on Sundays. Clueless about where these feelings came from, I decided to read books related to the pastor's sermons because the sermons alleviated my uneasiness. I was confused as to why I was fearful of the One whom I had just recently convinced myself did not exist.

Four weeks after I stopped attending church, I saw an advertisement in a local newspaper about an English Bible study at the YMCA. I was not interested in the Bible itself, but I did want to learn English. I tried to read the Bible several times during college, but I could not understand the contents at all. I could not read through even one chapter of the Old

7

Testament or New Testament. The Old Testament seemed full of ancient myths. The New Testament seemed to be full of unbelievable and unreasonable stories, such as the story of the virgin birth.

In any event, I went to the English Bible study class for the first time. It was held every Tuesday and Friday in the early evening. Two Canadian missionaries were the teachers. On my very first day, I was surprised to see an old friend from the same junior high school that I had attended.

Her face looked very happy and joyful, which came as a surprise. Years before, I had heard about her difficult situation from another friend. Her parents had passed away within three years of each other, and as the oldest child in the family, she had to take care of her six younger brothers and sisters. My friend was an elementary school teacher at that time. She rented a cheap place and tutored after school because her salary was not enough to support her family.

When I saw her happy face in the classroom, I thought she must be a much better Christian than I was because she had been faithfully attending church since childhood. We met again in the next class. After the Bible study, she came to me and said, "Sunja, we haven't seen each other for a long time. Why don't you join me downstairs for tea?"

For a while, we rambled on about ordinary things in our lives. Then she suddenly asked me a very peculiar question. "Sunja, if Jesus comes back tonight, are you sure that you will be saved?" When I heard such a strange question that no one had ever asked me before, I became suspicious of her faith. Her question did not make sense to me. I wondered whether she was part of a cult, such as the Jehovah's Witnesses or the Moonies.

Moreover, I had always believed that we would not be able to know who was saved or not until Christ's return. Who could be certain of one's salvation while living on this earth? I thought to myself, "She seemed like a good Christian, but what about me?" Many congregants in my church had complimented me on being a good Christian, so I answered her with a dismissive tone, "Well, maybe. God might save me because I have been attending church for a long time and have served the church in various ways."

My friend replied, "Sunja, it should not be a maybe. I have a conviction for my salvation right now."

I was deeply affected by her confident faith, and it led me to ponder her words for quite some time. Although her reply sounded strange, she seemed earnest. Should I listen to her idea of faith? Many books of proverbs advise us that "The wise listen to others' opinions, but the foolish never listen to others." So I asked her, "Would you tell me about the Jesus you believe in?"

I thought there was a different conception of faith between hers and mine. But instead of responding to my question, my friend said, "Sunja, I have peace in my heart. My mind is now focused on heaven." I was extremely surprised by her words because I had no peace at all. I only experienced anxiety, emptiness, and insecurity and had been nihilistic since my late teens.

I became humbled by her response and asked, "How did you become like that?" She suggested meeting a Bible teacher that she knew. A few days later, I met him with my friend. The teacher brought a big Bible and an old newspaper. He opened the Old Testament and showed me several prophecies for the Jews in the books of Deuteronomy, Jeremiah, and Ezekiel, where it predicted that they would lose their land.

> "If you do not carefully follow all the words of this law, which are written in this book, and do not revere this glorious and awesome name—the LORD your God— . . . **then the LORD will scatter you among all nations, from one end of the earth to the other.** There you will worship other gods—gods of wood and stone, which neither you nor your fathers have known." (Deuteronomy 28:58, 64, written in 1410–1395 BC, over 3,400 years ago.)

> The LORD said, "It is because they have forsaken my law, which I set before them; they have not obeyed me or followed my law. Instead, they have followed the stubbornness of their hearts; they have followed the Baals, as their fathers taught them." Therefore, this is what the LORD Almighty, the God of Israel, says: "See, I will make this people eat bitter food and drink poisoned water. **I will scatter them among nations** that neither they nor their fathers have known, and I will pursue them with the sword until I have destroyed them." (Jeremiah 9:13-16; Jeremiah prophesied in 627–580 BC, over 2,600 years ago.)

> **"I will disperse you among the nations and scatter you through the countries**, and I will put an end to your uncleanness." (Ezekiel 22:15)

Then the Bible teacher showed me prophecies about the Israelites that will return to their land.

> "This is what the Sovereign LORD says: **I will gather you from the nations and bring you back from the countries where you have been scattered**, and I will give you back the land of Israel again." (Ezekiel 11:17)

> "I will gather you from all the nations and places where I have banished you," declares the LORD, "**and will bring you back to the place from which I carried you into exile.**" (Jeremiah 29:14)

"For I will take you out of the nations; **I will gather you from all the countries and bring you back into your own land**." (Ezekiel 36:24)

"Then they will know that I am the LORD their God, for though I sent them into exile among the nations, **I will gather them to their own land**, not leaving any behind." (Ezekiel 39:28)

I had not known that those prophecies were in the Old Testament, which was written a long, long time ago. For the first time in my life, I discovered these historical, amazing prophecies from the books of the Bible. I felt that I had been blind to the Bible, but now I could see. It was really an awakening moment for me. All of God's prophecies have been exactly fulfilled thousands of years later. I had learned that the Jewish people lost their own land to the Romans in AD 70 and then came back into their land in AD 1948. Afterward, the teacher showed me an old newspaper article, which was written in 1967. It was a story about The Six Day War between Saudi Arabia and Israel from June 5 to 10. The war had taken place only two years before this. At that time, all the press of the world declared that Israel would be completely defeated by Saudi Arabia's huge army. However, the war came to an end with a huge victory for the Jews in just six short days to the utter surprise of the entire world.

According to the newspaper story, Israel fought with only 100 soldiers against 10,000 Arabian soldiers. After I read this news, the Bible teacher opened the Bible to Leviticus 26:8: "Five of you will chase a hundred, **and a hundred of you will chase ten thousand, and your enemies will fall by the sword before you**." As he finished reading this prophecy, I was amazed. It was written by the prophet Moses in about 1410–1395 BC. How would he be able to predict what would happen about 3,376 years later?

I thought that no one, not even the world's most famous fortune-teller, could predict so precisely as these prophecies. While I was attending college, many national newspapers reported that one of the most respected fortune-tellers of the world said that our earth would collapse in a month. But then nothing happened.

Through these amazing prophecies, I realized that there is an almighty God who directs and rules the history of the world. As soon as I acknowledged this fact, my heart (and my two knees) began to tremble with a strong fear in the presence of the Creator, the Lord. I felt that I was not ready to meet the holy and sovereign God yet. I was standing before God with both a dread of death and a fear of His punishment. "What must I do to be saved from His fearful judgment?" I could die at any moment by a sudden accident, a deadly disease, or a natural disaster. In fact, all of us, from the day of our birth, live each day with the possibility of death.

If I would die in a car accident on my way back home, I thought, Where would I go—hell or heaven? I asked the Bible teacher, "How can I be saved from the wrath of God?"

My soul was like a thirsty deer panting for streams of water. He opened to John 3 in the New Testament and read two verses. In verse three, Jesus declared, "I tell you the truth, no one can see the kingdom of God unless he is born again." And in verse five, Jesus said, "*I tell you the truth, no one can enter the kingdom of God unless he is born of water and the Spirit.*" I had not known these verses before. Now I could see these very important words that Jesus said to us over 1,900 years before. According to the Scriptures, *I must be born again of the Holy Spirit.*

I was really hungry for the Kingdom of God. I asked the teacher again, "How can I be born again of the Holy Spirit?" He read John 1:12: "To all who received him, to those who believed in his name, he gave the right to become children of God."

I inquired, "I'd like to know the way to receive Jesus Christ. Would you please explain how to receive Him?"

He said, "Open your heart."

I looked down at my heart, but I could not find a door. I really did not know how to open the door of my heart.

The next morning, I went to a Christian bookstore for the first time in my life. Before, I was not even remotely interested in Christian books. Now, I urgently wanted to know how to be born again of the Holy Spirit. I took a bus to go downtown. At the last bus stop on my way to the store, over ten people got on the bus, one by one. At that moment, I perceived them as dead people who were moving under the shadow of death, without life. I was also among them. Isaiah 9:2 describes this grave condition, "The people walking in darkness have seen a great light; **on those living in the land of the shadow of death** a light has dawned" (written in 745–680 BC).

When I arrived at the bookstore, I purchased a total of five books. *Peace with God* and *World Aflame* were both written by Billy Graham, and the other three books were written by a Canadian pastor, including *The Most Loving Country*. I started to read these books with great focus and finished all of them in six days. All these books only reiterated that we need to be born again of the Holy Spirit in order to enter the Kingdom of God. The problem was that they did not mention the specific way to be born again.

My friend had given me a book called *The Pilgrim's Progress* by John Bunyan, which, apart from the Bible, is one of the most beloved classic Christian books in history. I had tried to read this book before, but it was too hard to understand. However, this time I was able to understand that the meaningful story related to sin and the cross. While the book was not hard to understand, I still could not see how the cross of Jesus was connected to me as it was to others.

In the meantime, my friend called me and said, "Why don't you meet a missionary from Holland? He is now living in the city of Taejon. He helped me so that I might be born again of the Holy Spirit." I complied with great enthusiasm, hungry to learn how I might come to experience this.

It would take only two hours to get there by train. I thought to myself, "I wish I could go to see Jesus Christ Himself, even if He lives at the end of the earth. So I'll go and see the missionary and hope for the best."

The next morning, my friend and I went to the Taegu train station. When I arrived, I saw that many people in the station were walking without life under the shadow of death. It was the same image as I saw before on the bus. I felt so sorry once again that I was among them.

It was lunchtime when we arrived in Taejon. My friend took me to a young couple's home. They were living in one small room and seemed poor. They cooked a meager lunch of one simple bowl of kimchi noodle soup. Yet they looked so happy and peaceful in their faith in Jesus. I envied their confident and peaceful demeanor.

After a late lunch, we went to the missionary's house in the suburbs. The missionary and his wife had gone to visit another family. There were only three children with a babysitter. While we were waiting for them, my friend kept on talking to me, but I could not pay attention to her. My only concern was meeting the missionary. I wanted to see him as soon as possible because of my zealous desire to be born again. He was my hope.

After a while, the entrance door opened, and the missionary and his wife were standing there with big smiles for us. At that moment, the Holy Spirit opened up a vision of spiritual reality. I saw a brilliant light surrounding them, but I was wearing unclean clothes.

They walked toward us, but I could not look at them directly because I felt like a dirty sinner before them. Feeling sinful was new to me. Ever since my childhood, I was used to hearing that I was a good person from my parents, kin, and many of my close friends. I had been proud of myself in terms of my character, at least. I realized that I was clean in the sight of men, but I was not so in the sight of God.

After the missionary listened to my friend about my pursuit of salvation, he said to me, "Read Exodus, not only as a history of the Jews but also as a spiritual interpretation." Then they went into their room.

I expected a lot from him, but that was all he said. I was disappointed. With nothing else said, I began to read Exodus. It was late evening. When I finished all of Exodus, the sun was beginning to rise. As I wrote before, I had tried to read the Old Testament in the past, but I could not understand it at all. However, that night, I understood the contents of the whole book without any difficulty or boredom. This was a remarkable transformation in me.

I understood that the Red Sea, which the Israelites passed through to get

12

away from the Egyptian army symbolized the blood of Jesus. When they passed through the Red Sea, it was an exodus from the slavery of Egypt. In the New Testament, this meant the blood of Jesus Christ was an exodus from the slavery of the law of sin and death. The Israelites' forty years of living in the wilderness represents the life of Christians in this world. Crossing over the Jordan River symbolizes a genuine Christian's farewell from this world to heaven.

Later, I read the same interpretation as confirmed by other Christian books. However, my mind and soul didn't have any feeling of salvation. My knowledge was correct, but my heart was not in the right place.

At this point, everybody else in the house was still sleeping. I was looking out the window at a field covered by snow. "Where is God? I have not been able to find Him, but He should know where I am. I hope that some miracle comes upon me from God." I felt that I was standing alone before God, who was still invisible to me. No one could help me to meet God; not my Christian parents, not my born-again friend, not even the missionary from whom I had expected the most. I experienced total solitude before God. I wept and quietly began to sing hymns that reflected the feelings in my heart: "**Father, I stretch my hands to Thee; No other help I know. If Thou withdraw Thyself from me, Oh! whither shall I go?**"[1] I also sang, "**Jesus, Savior, pilot me, Over life's tempestuous sea,** Unknown waves before me roll, Hiding rocks and treach'rous shoal; Chart and compass come from Thee— **Jesus, Savior, pilot me!**[2] Amen."

. While I was singing, I kept weeping with a broken heart. I could not sleep at all. My eyes became swollen that Sunday morning. After breakfast, we went to the missionary's office. We had a worship service there with about fifteen to twenty people. During the worship service, I was in tears. I could not concentrate on his sermon because I was so disappointed by the missionary that I was losing hope that I could ever be born again of the Holy Spirit. I had strong expectations from our visit. Yet I had not received any special insight from him. His sole advice was to read Exodus.

After the service, the missionary called me. He saw me weeping while the worship service was going on. I sat by him. He knelt down on the bare floor and prayed for me deeply for a while. Then he said to me, "No matter how skilled or famous a gynecologist is, he still must wait ten months for a fetus to grow in a mother's womb. Growing a baby is God's work. Your birth seems near." When I heard what he was saying, I realized that I had trusted in famous pastors and missionaries instead of God Himself for my salvation. I recognized that I had gone the wrong way. Until this point, I had been walking in the wrong direction. So with great conviction, I decided from that point on that I would trust in God only. Even though He still felt out of touch from my heart, I strongly believed in His presence.

Through the missionary's words, I gained clear hope. I thanked him so much for my new inspiration to continue my search for God. While I was thinking about this matter, suddenly one young man shouted to me while holding up a big Bible in his hand, "Do you believe this Bible is God's book?" I thought, *Oh, my goodness! Is that Bible God's book?* At that moment, I recognized that I had not believed the Bible was literally the words of God himself. I realized that I had thought of the Bible simply as a good moral book.

I realized, "Oh, this Bible's real author is God!" Very strangely, without conscious will or reason, from that moment on I became convinced that the Bible was God's own words. When I was traveling back home on the train, I considered my future plans regarding searching for God. From now on, I will trust in God only, even though I do not know where He is. He will know who I am and where I am. I will read the Bible as God's textbook or letter for me. God is my teacher. I am His student. I will learn from the greatest Teacher through the Bible. I remembered two of God's verses that were very popular in my church.

Ask and it will be given to you; seek and you will find; knock and the door will be opened to you. (Matthew 7:7)

By day you led them with a pillar of cloud, and by night with a pillar of fire to give them light on the way they were to take. (Nehemiah 9:12)

According to God's Word, I had been seeking God and asking God to be born again of the Holy Spirit. I trusted that eventually, God would answer me. I also believed a great holy light would direct me in the way I should go.

After I got back home, the next morning I went to work as a teaching assistant at the national university. After I finished my work, I went to my office and opened a Christian journal, *The Life of Success*, which I brought from the office of the missionary. I began to read. I loved to read Scripture on the top section of each page rather than the main subject in it, and then I found the testimony of Martin Luther. I wanted to read his story because he was a very famous Reformer in the world of Christianity after the Middle Ages. He had struggled valiantly in order to receive the assurance of salvation.

From Martin Luther's story, I learned that God's salvation is not through men's good deeds or achievements for God but through faith alone in Christ's finished work. Martin Luther could not gain the assurance of salvation through his fasting and ascetic practices. He finally found his conviction of salvation by God's words: "But my righteous one will live by faith" (Hebrews 10:38).

God's Word struck his heart by the Holy Spirit so that this monk and professor of theology came to realize where God's salvation comes from.

For it is by grace you have been saved, through faith—and this is not from yourselves, it is the gift of God—not by works, so that no one can boast. (Ephesians 2:8-9)

Still, my mind was the same as before. Nothing had changed. I just understood his story. In fact, while I was searching for God, I had only been eating a little bit. This was partly because I had lost my appetite, but I was also choosing to limit my food because I wanted to earn God's compassion toward me. After I read Luther's testimony, I knew those kinds of deeds were useless before God. So I packed up my work bag and went home.

I ate well for the first time since I started to search for God. After dinner, I had to meet someone, so I didn't get to sit at my desk to read the Bible until late in the evening. It was February 11, 1969. I was twenty-five years old.

3
INEXPRESSIBLE JOY, EVERLASTING LIFE

It was eleven o'clock at night, and I had just returned from a date with the man who would become my husband. I was sleepy, so I doused my face with cold water to awaken myself so I could spend my late-night hours reading God's Word. Because my friend recommended to me the Gospel of John, I began with that book and put a new notebook on the desk. I grabbed a pen and started to read from the first page.

Before I started to read, I said to myself that this Bible is God's letter to me. If my earthly father sent me a letter, I would read it very carefully. Therefore, I will read my heavenly Father's letter with even more attention. I really wanted to know what God was saying in this book. I began to read from the first verse with complete and total concentration. I was amazed at how different the Bible was from that moment on. The book of John was not boring or difficult anymore but was so easy to understand. I read for two straight hours until I came to John 14:6. The verse arrested my heart! Jesus said, "I am the way [to God] and the truth and the life [God's eternal life]. No one comes to the Father except through me."

I excitedly responded in my heart, "Oh! Is Jesus Christ the only way to God? Does no one come to the Father except through Jesus Christ?" I realized I had been thinking that I could go to heaven through my good works and attending church with great devotion. However, Jesus Christ provided a totally different way to redemption than mine. I had never realized that no one comes to the heavenly Father except through Jesus Christ because I had not understood God's words before. My heart cried out to God, "What shall I do now?" Did I have to reject my own ideas of salvation for God's truth?

That night, I had to decide whether I would accept this declaration from Jesus Christ or not. I had believed in God's presence and that the Bible was written by the Holy Spirit through all this process of my spiritual journey. I knew later that the Holy Spirit had already come into my heart to guide and teach me. But at the time, I opened my notebook and began to draw a description of what I was learning.

A Clear Path between God and Humans

Now the LORD God had planted a garden in the east, in Eden; and there he put the man he had formed. (Genesis 2:8)

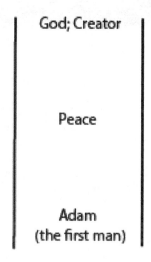

God created Adam and Eve. He blessed and loved them. There was peace, joy, happiness, and love between God and them.

However, later, Adam and Even listened to Satan's words rather than God's command. They chose Satan's lie instead of their Creator's truth. As a result of their incorrect choice, God drove them out of the Garden Paradise and put barriers between God and humankind. Thus, my illustration changed.

A Barrier between God and Humans

Because you . . . ate from the tree about which I commanded you, "You must not eat of it," Cursed is the ground because of you; through painful toil you will eat of it all the days of your life. (Genesis 3:17)

Therefore, just as sin entered the world through one man, and death through sin, and in this way death came to all men, because all sinned. (Romans 5:12)

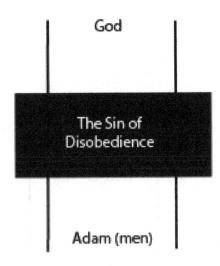

Human beings were separated from God's presence until Jesus Christ came as our Savior and Redeemer. The prophet Isaiah predicted this hundreds of years before Christ's birth: "Therefore the Lord himself will give you a sign: **The virgin will be with child and will give birth to a son, and will call him Immanuel [which means, God with us]**" (Isaiah 7:14, 750– 700 BC).

> He [Jesus] himself is our peace, who has made the two one and has
> destroyed the barrier, the dividing wall of hostility, by abolishing in
> his flesh the law with its commandments and regulations. His
> purpose was to create in himself one new man out of the two, thus
> making peace. (Ephesians 2:14-15)

We were all dead in the sight of God when the first man, Adam, committed the sin of disobedience. The barrier of sin between God and mankind had separated us from God's presence. Therefore, we could not see God or even perceive Him. So God planned our redemption from the beginning, before Adam and Eve were driven out of Eden. The apostle Paul wrote in Ephesians 1:4, 7-8: "For he chose us in him before the creation of the world to be holy and blameless in his sight. ... In him we have redemption through his blood, the forgiveness of sins, in accordance with the riches of God's grace that he lavished on us."

Thousands of years after Adam's rebellion, God sent His one and only Son, Jesus Christ, to redeem human beings in this world. Jesus Christ, the Son of God, paid back to God the wages of Adam's sin through His death according to God's law. As the prophet John said, "Look, the Lamb of God, who takes away the sin of the world!" (John 1:29).

Jesus' Sacrifice

Through him to reconcile to himself all things, whether things on earth or things in heaven, by making peace through his blood, shed on the cross. (Colossians 1:20)

He was pierced for our transgressions, he was crushed for our iniquities; the punishment that brought us peace was upon him, and by his wounds we are healed. . . . The LORD has laid on him the iniquity of us all. (Isaiah 53:5-6)

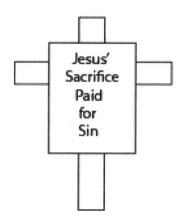

Jesus shed His blood for the world. As the Scripture says:

"The law requires that nearly everything be cleansed with blood, and without the shedding of blood there is no forgiveness" (Hebrews 9:22).

"For the life of a creature is in the blood, and I have given it to you to make atonement for yourselves on the altar; it is the blood that makes atonement for one's life." (Leviticus 17:11)

Jesus Christ gave us the key to heaven's gate. At last, the way to heaven opened through His son's sacrificial, cruel death. Jesus Christ paid off the debt of our sins to God with His holy blood.

"For as in Adam all die, so in Christ all will be made alive." (1 Corinthians 15:22)

"For the wages of sin is death, but the gift of God is eternal life in Christ Jesus our Lord." (Romans 6:23)

The Clear Path between God and Humans Restored through Christ

Therefore there is now no condemnation for those who are in Christ Jesus, because through Christ Jesus the law of the Spirit of life set me free from the law of sin and death. (Romans 8:1-2)

But now he has reconciled you by Christ's physical body through death to present you holy in his sight, without blemish and free from accusation. (Colossians 1:22)

Everyone who believes in Him may have eternal life.

Now this is eternal life: that they may know you, the only true God, and Jesus Christ, whom you have sent. (John 17:3)

This is the LORD, we trusted in him; let us rejoice and be glad in his salvation. (Isaiah 25:9)

God said that Jesus Christ, who is the Creator's only Son, is the only way to heaven. Through all these explanations of the Holy Spirit, our spiritual counselor, I had an inner dialogue:

"Sunja, when Jesus Christ took the sins of the whole world on the cross, do you believe He took everyone else's sins except yours?"
"No, I don't think so."
"Sunja, where do you live, in the world or out of the world?"
"I live in the world."
"Then can you believe that Jesus took your sins as well when He shed His blood on the cross about 2,000 years ago in Jerusalem?"

"Yes, I can."

"Do you think God is a liar?"

"No, not at all. God's prophecies for the Jews were fulfilled exactly about 3,500 years later. Therefore, I trust God and believe His words are truth."

"Do you think some portion of the Bible is not true?"

"No, I believe that the whole book of the Bible is God's perfect book written under the inspiration of the Holy Spirit. Also, it would be extremely hard to identify which part is true or not. It is better for me to believe all the words were written by the inspiration of God's Spirit. In other words, all the messages came from God's mouth."

"Then you must believe in God's salvation through the blood of Jesus Christ alone."

"Yes, I can't help but believe that Jesus Christ is my Savior, my Redeemer from sin and death."

I decided to accept Jesus Christ as my Savior. So I knelt down on the floor and prayed to God, "Dear God, I'll accept Your Son, Jesus Christ, as my Savior. I believe that Jesus cleansed away my sins as well as the world's sin by His blood on the cross. I pray in the name of Jesus, amen."

After the prayer, I was so tired. It was almost two o'clock in the morning. I laid down on the bed, but I soon got up again. I was restless because I expected some joy would come into my heart after my prayer, like my friend's joyful face. However, my heart had not experienced any of this joy. It made me wonder if I just perceived Jesus as an historical truth. I knelt down and prayed again:

Dear God, You said in the Bible: "To all who received him, to those who believed in his name, he gave the right to become children of God" (John 1:12). By Your words, I received and believed Jesus Christ as my Savior tonight. But why do I not feel any joy or conviction of being Your child? I imagine that if the queen of the United Kingdom had a little daughter, the girl would realize one day that she is a princess of a big country, and she would be so incredibly happy! Now, I just became a princess of the King of all kings, according to Your promise. Why do I not have any feelings of deep joy or happiness, or any assurance of this salvation? Dear God, would You please give me some evidence that I became Your daughter?

As soon as my prayer finished, I began to experience something miraculous. I had never undergone such an amazing supernatural experience in my life. I felt my tongue become a bit heavy without my will. Then it pulled back a tiny bit inside my mouth, and my tongue began to move around by itself. Then I heard the most beautiful, sweet, loving, and meek voice, unlike anything I had ever heard from a human. It sounded divine and repeated out loud three times, "Oh, Lord, thank You! Oh, Lord, thank You! Oh, Lord, thank You!" My tongue was not mine, but the Holy Spirit's at that moment! The voice was beyond description, but hearing the wondrous voice, I thought that whoever owned it would never become angry or shout at others until the day of their death. I would never be able to imitate this sweet voice, no matter how hard I tried, because it was not like any human voice. At that moment, I realized by the sound of His voice that the character of God is love itself, far beyond our wildest imagination. I immediately stood up and lifted my hands in the air and shouted with amazing joy, because at that moment, I had met the King of kings who is the Creator of the whole world!

"O God, You are right here in this room. I had no idea you were with me right now. I always thought You were far away from me. O God! I'm alive now!" At that moment, I felt God's infinite, everlasting life connecting with my short, finite life, overflowing into my body. God gave me a conviction by His specific words, which I hadn't known, through His divine tongue. I heard the Lord say to me, "I have justified you. Who is he that condemns you? You have crossed over from death to life."

When I heard His words, I knew I had finally crossed over from death to life. I was assured at that moment that I had received God's eternal life! I did not need to be fearful of my death anymore! Inexpressible joy in my victory exploded out of me! "This is the happiest moment of my life! I got the whole world! I now have total satisfaction with an eternal guarantee."

Sometime later, I found these same words in the Bible, in John 5:24 and Romans 8:33. It was a miracle for me to hear God's words now, which were from Jesus Christ and the apostle Paul, written under the inspiration of the Holy Spirit around 2,000 years ago.

"Oh, my Lord, Your salvation is so simple and easy. I had thought salvation was very difficult, requiring much human striving and good deeds. But now, I found that Your salvation needs only faith in what You prepared for us through Jesus Christ."

Jesus said, "The work of God is this: to believe in the one he has sent." (John 6:29)

I am the resurrection and the life. He who believes in me will live, even though he dies; and whoever lives and believes in me will never die. (John 11:25-26)

For God so loved the world that he gave his one and only Son, that whoever believes in him shall not perish but have eternal life. (John 3:16)

Jesus paid our debt of sin in Jerusalem; therefore, we do not need to do anything for our salvation, which is from God, not from us. So I told God again, "Oh, Lord, what marvelous news from heaven! Our salvation is so easy to get. You prepared all for us. I will tell everybody that Your salvation is a free gift from the death and resurrection of Jesus Christ. I will invite them to come and freely take their citizenship in heaven by faith alone in Jesus Christ, our Savior."

As Scripture says, "This is love: not that we loved God, but that he loved us and sent his Son as an atoning sacrifice for our sins" (1 John 4:10).

Through God's miraculous and gracious guidance, I obtained eternal happiness and satisfaction. I felt like dancing all night as a redeemed person. I was not able to sleep because it felt like I was in heaven. I could not contain the exhilaration, so I began to sing hymns throughout the night. As I sang, I realized for the first time that these hymns were written by Christians who were also born of the Holy Spirit. Before, I had sung hymns as if they were school songs or oldies; I did not reflect on the meaning of the words. But God opened my spiritual eyes. So all the hymns I sang were just expressions of my mind.

If God had asked me that night, "What do you want Me to do?" I would have answered, "You did everything for me that I had needed and wanted." God's amazing grace has been overflowing in my soul. Thank you, Lord! I began to sing, "Amazing grace (how sweet the sound) that saved a wretch like me! I once was lost, but now am found, was blind, but now I see."[1] The Holy Spirit had converted my eyes into spiritual eyes that now perceived God. As I continued to sing hymns into the night, I proclaimed, "Blessed assurance, Jesus is mine! Oh, what a foretaste of glory divine! Heir of salvation, purchase of God, born of his Spirit, washed in his blood."[2]

> I delight greatly in the LORD; my soul rejoices in my God. For he has clothed me with garments of salvation and arrayed me in a robe of righteousness, as a bridegroom adorns his head like a priest, and as a bride adorns herself with her jewels. (Isaiah 61:10)

Through this previous experience, I understood the reason why the Holy Spirit spoke through me in tongues, saying "Oh, Lord, thank You!" three times. Before, when I confessed to God that I had received Jesus as my Savior, I had to say, "Oh, Lord, thank You for giving me Your salvation freely," but I did not. Instead, I only requested a sign. So the Holy Spirit dwelling in me gave thanks to God in my place. "The Counselor, the Holy Spirit, whom the Father will send in my name, will teach you all things and will remind you of everything I have said to you" (John 14:26).

The next morning, I met my other Christian friend. I said to her without thinking, "I became a righteous person last night." She was so surprised at what I told her that she stared at me, speechless. As I shared my testimony with her, I sensed the Lord purify my heart, and it felt as pure as a newborn baby's skin. I realized my dirty heart was thoroughly washed by the precious blood of Jesus Christ.

"Come now, let us reason together," says the LORD. "Though your sins are like scarlet, they shall be as white as snow; though they are red as crimson, they shall be like wool." (Isaiah 1:18)

Since that day, I became a passionate evangelist. As I described earlier, while I was seeking God in my own way, God had not answered at all because I wasn't looking for God in the way He promised we would find Him. The Scripture says, "You have been born again, not of perishable seed, but of imperishable, through the living and enduring word of God" (1 Peter 1:23). God chose to wait until I stopped insisting on finding Him my own way, through signs and wonders, rather than looking for Him in His enduring Word. As soon as I let go of my way, as if God Himself was waiting, He immediately came to guide me to His living water.

My way of seeking took three years without any reward, but God's way to direct me took only eleven days. God's immense grace and wisdom followed me until I met Him. God had adopted me as a princess of the Kingdom of God through the help of God's Spirit.

I often say, "I am one of the most successful people in the world because I became the daughter of the King of all kings!" While I was seeking God for three years, I had asked Him to give me at least one clear sign of His existence: allowing me to speak in tongues, giving me a holy vision, or healing my intestines. However, God did not give me any of them when I tried to seek Him my way. And yet, amazingly, God gave me all three signs after I believed in God and Jesus Christ, through God's words. I experienced the truth of James 1:5, that "God . . . gives generously to all without finding fault."

First, He healed my intestines. About one week after being born again, I found I could eat meals very well, even a full bowl of rice. I was so amazed by my healthy digestion. For six years, I could not eat even half a bowl of my meal. Since then, my intestines have worked well without any problems, all by the grace of God!

Second, I experienced the Holy Spirit. I had already experienced the divine tongues when the Holy Spirit came to me after receiving Jesus Christ as my Savior, saying, "Oh, Lord, thank you!" three times. However, God's grace was overflowing in me as I experienced divine tongues again. About four years later, in October of 1973, my friend visited me. She had already received the gift of tongues. Before she left my home, she prayed in tongues that I could not understand. After I took her to the bus stop, I came back home and prayed, "Dear Father, I really envy my friend. I would like to speak in tongues too! So I ask You to give me the gift of tongues like her. Please, Father. I pray in Jesus' name, amen."

Immediately after finishing my prayer, I received an extraordinary sign. I began to speak in tongues. While I was speaking, my eyes filled with tears and my heart felt deeply troubled and pained. I could not understand what the Holy Spirit was saying in this strange language. It was none of the world's languages that I had any familiarity with. It was clear to me that this was a divine tongue of the Holy Spirit. Then I asked God about the troubled way I was feeling. "God, why am I weeping with a painful heart? I want to understand what You are saying to me." I had read in the New Testament about the ability to interpret divine tongues. So I asked God once more, "Would You give me an interpretation for this tongue?" As it says in the Scripture, 'Anyone who speaks in a tongue should pray that he may interpret what he says' (1 Corinthians 14:13)."

He did not answer until I had made seven or eight heartfelt requests. Eventually, He responded to my pleas. He began to interpret in Korean with an accent that sounded like the speaker was an American or European missionary in Korea. I excitedly thought, "Wow! The Holy Spirit knows Korean! What an awesome God! God must know every language in the world!" The Holy Spirit said to me, "While you don't love your mother truly, whom you can see, yet you say you love God, whom you have not seen. Your lips are detestable."

When I heard this translation, I was astonished. I had been living with my mother-in-law since I got married, so I was perplexed as to which mother God wanted me to love. All that was clear was that I needed to love them from the depths of my heart. I perceived that I had treated them pretty well, but I knew that it was not to the extent that God commanded: "Love your neighbor as yourself" (Matthew 22:39). Since I received God's instruction, I put my effort and prayer toward practicing love from my heart for others.

Later, when I began to read the whole New Testament, I found the words from my experience of speaking in tongues in 1 John 4:20, "If anyone says, 'I love God,' yet hates his brother, he is a liar. For anyone who does not love his brother, whom he has seen, cannot love God, whom he has not seen." Those were the exact words that God had spoken through me in tongues, even though I had never read that verse in my life! I was so amazed when I read this verse in the Bible that God had spoken through me in tongues before, and I recognized that I had experienced a direct communication with God through the words written almost 2,000 years before by the apostle John, who was under the inspiration of the Holy Spirit.

Since that event, I have been praying in tongues, even singing in tongues with hymns that God brings to me that are perfect for my situation. When I worry about something distressing, God comforts me by letting my tongue sing hymns that lift me out of my anxious heart. One of the hymns the Spirit often brings to my tongue is one about trust:

> The trusting heart to Jesus clings,
> Nor any ill forebodes,
> But at the cross of Calv'ry sings,
> Praise God for lifted loads!
> Singing, I go along life's road,
> Praising the Lord, praising the Lord;
> Singing, I go along life's road,
> For Jesus has lifted my load.[3]

Soon after, the Holy Spirit spoke to me. "Do you think I didn't hear your prayer asking for the three signs of tongues, visions, and healing in the revival services? Of course I heard your requests, but I did not give them to you while you were in those services. I wanted to let you know that I am not present in those kinds of noisy, disorderly places, as was written in the Scriptures, 'God is not a God of disorder but of peace' (1 Corinthians 14:33)."

4
A SPIRITUAL VISION OF JESUS

A week after being born again, I had a dream while I slept. In it, I looked up and saw the bright face of Jesus Christ. It was the final day of human history, and Jesus was returning as the King of all kings. The sky was full of the face of Jesus. His face was full of rejoicing and overflowed with happiness, peace, truth, and love beyond description. I thought, "Wow! Jesus is perfect in His beauty!"

Then an angel who looked like a thin man came to my younger sister and me. He was trying to take my sister first, but soon after, he took me instead. Then he flew with me into the air for a while and put me in something that resembled a temporary holding area.

I looked around, but I saw only a small group of people. I was trying to find my family members among them, but I could not find any. Then I awakened from my dream. I was certain I would be saved when the end of the ages came. I also realized that God wanted me to testify about my journey of salvation to my family as soon as possible. So, I went up to Seoul where my family lived and shared with them how to be born again.

In order to witness effectively to my family, I needed to review the steps by which God led me to be born again. With the help of my guide, the Holy Spirit, I met my Father, whom I had been seeking. Scripture says, "Those who seek me find me" (Proverbs 8:17). First, God had to give me an assurance of His existence. Second, He gave me a deep conviction that the Bible is God's Word. Third, God enabled me to read His words very carefully, which led me to know Jesus. Fourth, by graciously giving me faith to believe and accept Jesus Christ as my own Savior, I could be reunited with God and establish an intimate, familiar relationship with God as my heavenly Father and me as His beloved daughter. In the same way, anyone can become God's child if that person would follow a similar process.

Being born again of the Holy Spirit is a simple concept. The essence is not based on wondrous signs or feelings but occurs solely by faith in Jesus Christ alone. As Jesus said, "Whoever **believes** in him shall not perish but have eternal life" (John 3:16). The apostle Paul wrote, "You are all sons of God **through faith** in Christ Jesus" (Galatians 3:26). And Paul also wrote, "We have been justified **through faith**" (Romans 5:1).

Therefore, if you believe in God and Jesus Christ and are baptized in the name of Jesus, the Holy Spirit will come into your cleansed heart by the shed blood of Jesus Christ. I encountered the Holy Spirit very dramatically, but some will have a more gradual experience. Regardless, God is still inviting us to Himself through His Word: "Listen, listen to me, and eat what is good, and your soul will delight in the richest of fare" (Isaiah 55:2).

If you are concerned about heaven and hell and are not yet saved, please persist in asking God to give you faith in Christ because our faith comes from above, not from our will. Never hesitate to ask for this gift from God. Our eternal life with God is the most valuable gift from God. As He says in Jeremiah 33:3, "Call to me and I will answer you and tell you great and unsearchable things you do not know."

There are two kinds of people in the sight of God: Those who are blind and those who can see; those who are dead and those who are alive. I love this Bible story:

> As Jesus approached Jericho, a blind man was sitting by the roadside begging. When he heard the crowd going by, he asked what was happening. They told him, "Jesus of Nazareth is passing by." He called out, "Jesus, Son of David, have mercy on me!" Those who led the way rebuked him and told him to be quiet, but he shouted all the more, "Son of David, have mercy on me!" Jesus stopped and ordered the man to be brought to him. When he came near, Jesus asked him, "What do you want me to do for you?" "Lord, I want to see," he replied. Jesus said to him, "Receive your sight; your faith has healed you." Immediately he received his sight and followed Jesus, praising God. When all the people saw it, they also praised God. (Luke 18:35-43)

Through this story, we can discover several truths. First, the blind man was fully aware of his inability to see. When a child is born blind, the child is not usually aware of their difference from others. They have not yet discerned that there are people who can see the world. However, the blind man was cognizant of his blindness. Before we can be born again, we must come to recognize that we are all spiritually blind from birth.

Second, the blind man knew who Jesus was and believed that Jesus was able to heal him.

Third, he shouted and shouted even louder despite the crowd's displeasure. In the face of opposition, he was determined because he had the conviction that Jesus could restore his sight. When Jesus saw his faith, He asked him, "What do you want me to do for you?" Can you imagine if He asked you that? How would you respond? Would you ask for health or financial prosperity? Maybe you might ask for a spouse or children. However, what is most important is what is eternal. As Paul wrote, "So we fix our eyes not on what is seen, but on what is unseen. For what is seen is temporary, but what is unseen is eternal" (2 Corinthians 4:18).

In the future, all of us will see the Son of God sitting at the right hand of the Father, in whom we have redemption and forgiveness of sins. Instead of asking for temporary things, would you consider praying something like this:

Dear God, I am going to read Your Word to learn Your will, but it can be very hard to understand. I feel spiritually blind to You. Please help me to see You through Your holy Scriptures, and lead me in Your way. I desperately want to be reunited with You in Your everlasting presence. I pray in the name of Jesus, amen.

After you pray this, I would encourage you to read the Gospel of John first and then Romans, which I believe is the crown jewel of the New Testament. After that, choose whatever book you would like. While you are reading, pay particularly close attention to Jesus, who is the main focus throughout the whole Bible.

The main purpose of the Old Testament is to anticipate the coming of Jesus as the Messiah. The New Testament is all about Jesus, who is the fulfillment of the Old Testament promises. It may help you to join a local Bible study in a Bible-believing, Christ-centered church to facilitate your understanding of the Bible. I want to reiterate that the most important issue is whether your goal is eternity or this temporary life. I humbly plead with you to choose heaven! In the last book of the Bible, it is written, "If anyone's name was not found written in the **book of life**, he was thrown into the lake of fire" (Revelation 20:15).

May our eternal Father's grace and guidance be with you always!

5
WHY IS CHRISTIANITY SO EXCLUSIVE?

It was just before our family moved to Chicago from Berkeley, California, in 1983. I was leading a Bible study group that consisted of about thirteen PhD students' wives who would gather weekly in my house. During one meeting, we had an unexpected visitor. Her husband was a professor from the top university in Korea—Seoul National—and was a visiting exchange professor at UC Berkeley. She possessed a brilliant mind, and she had graduated from the top women's college in Korea where she had majored in English Literature, one of the most competitive majors to get into. As I led the group through a study of the Gospel of John, she abruptly interrupted: "Why is Christianity so exclusive? Why is it such a self-righteous religion compared to other world religions like Buddhism? Other religions are not as exclusive as Christianity but are more inclusive of others." I could feel the eyes of the whole group eagerly looking at me, curious to hear how I would respond. They all wanted to know the answer to this question, as they, too, had wondered about it.

I had never studied theology, so I couldn't rely on any previous knowledge. I simply had my dependence on the Holy Spirit along with the holy Scriptures. Initially, I did not know how to respond, but in a quick second, God gave me an answer that I knew was from Him. The words popped into my mind, "It is a matter of being born again!" Even though I had never considered the question before, I began to give an explanation by God's inspiration. "If you believe in our Creator as your God, you must trust in His instructions in the Bible, which was written by the Spirit of God. Jesus Christ said in the Bible, 'I tell you the truth, no one can enter the Kingdom of God unless he is born of water and the Spirit. Flesh gives birth to flesh, but the Spirit gives birth to spirit' (John 3:5-6)." I asked her, "Why have you attended church so far? Do you want to enter the Kingdom of God instead of hell? Then you must be born again of the Holy Spirit as Jesus has said.

Otherwise, you can never enter the Kingdom of God. If God said that we could go to heaven through our good deeds, we could then, of course, be like other religions and admit people like they do. That's because those religions guide people toward living a moral and righteous life so that they can go to a better place after death. However, when God talks about our 'new birth,' it is a completely different concept altogether. Our amazing God wants to transform us from Adam's sinful nature into God's holy nature. In fact, the Bible teaches: 'For just as through the disobedience of the one man the many were made sinners, so also through the obedience of the one man the many will be made righteous' (Romans 5:19). What God is saying through this verse is that while the blood of Adam produces sinners, the blood of Jesus Christ gives birth to righteousness. Now then, what must we do to be born again of the Holy Spirit? Jesus said, 'Yet to all who received him, to those who believed in his name, he gave the right to become children of God—children born not of natural descent, nor of human decision or a husband's will, but born of God' (John 1:12-13). Additionally, the apostle Peter said, 'Repent and be baptized, every one of you, in the name of Jesus Christ for the forgiveness of your sins. And you will receive the gift of the Holy Spirit' (Acts 2:38). According to God's Word, we should first come back to Him from pursuing our own way and receive Jesus Christ as our personal Savior. Then the blood of Jesus will cleanse our filthy hearts and the Holy Spirit will come into our pure hearts to dwell with us forever. In this way, we are born again of the Holy Spirit as a child of God. Our rebirth comes from God's Holy Spirit in our hearts by faith through accepting Jesus Christ as our personal Savior, and not by Buddha or another god. Therefore, God tells us through His Word that in regard to Jesus, 'Salvation is found in no one else, for there is no other name under heaven given to men by which we must be saved' (Acts 4:12)."

After I finished reading these Scripture passages as an explanation to answer her question, there was a momentary silence, and God was clearly touching people's hearts. No one objected to my explanation. Because of this, I was able to pray in my heart, "Dear wonderful Father, thank You so much for the honor of sharing Your wisdom with me. I could have received disgrace in this situation, but instead, You honored me by giving me wisdom when I had no answer. Because of Your presence with me, I was able to answer them with Your Word, and bring honor to Your name. I pray this in the name of Jesus, amen."

She continued to come to the Bible study in the weeks to come. Eventually, she and her husband returned to Korea. Later, she was diagnosed with leukemia. When she heard I was visiting Korea, she invited many friends to her house so that I could share the gospel with them as well. As far as I could tell, she had put her faith in Jesus, and she is now rejoicing with the only true and living God!

6

BORN-AGAIN TRANSFORMATION

As the Bible became clearly understandable, I found all the answers to my search in it. Particularly, Matthew 5–7 became my spiritual food for my new character. I tried to put those precious words into practice in my daily life with the help of the Holy Spirit. Jesus says, "It is written: Man does not live on bread alone, but on every word that comes from the mouth of God" (Matthew 4:4).

I used to be fond of reading many books, fiction and non-fiction, especially romantic love stories and mysteries. I also enjoyed movies. However, after my rebirth, I became mostly interested in reading the Bible and Christian books and sometimes nonfiction as well. God's amazing words caused my spirit to grow healthy and truthful. I made efforts to correct my improper behaviors according to God's words. My concept of sin had changed, and some acts that I had not considered sinful were revealed as sins in the sight of God.

The Holy Spirit wanted me to be holy like our heavenly Father. I realized that I had many kinds of internal sins that were against God's teachings. I started to seek God's glory rather than my own, as I do not love earthly things more than God and His will.

> But the Counselor, the Holy Spirit, whom the Father will send in my name, will teach you all things and will remind you of everything I have said to you. (John 14:26)

Here are some examples of how the Holy Spirit began to correct my sinful nature.

The first story came a month after my rebirth. God's Spirit began working on my gossiping tongue. In the early afternoon, I was percolating some coffee for a coffee break for professors in our department's main office. After a time, my chief professor left the office. As soon as she left the room, four young professors began to gossip behind her back. As I was listening to them, the Holy Spirit touched my heart to teach me the way I should go. Before I was born again, I would join in with them because we all felt that our boss deserved it. She was mean and had a strong personality, which made us stressed. If she was with us, we were always on edge, so I never felt guilt for gossiping about her. However, this time, the Holy Spirit told me quietly, "Those who speak ill of others commit a greater sin than the one whom they talk about." This was the first time I learned about gossip being a sin. Since then, I have tried not to speak ill of other's weak points.

Another time in which the Holy Spirit corrected me, ironically, was while I was trying to correct myself. I would often be disappointed at my persistent failures. I really wanted to be a good example of a Christ follower to my unbelieving friends, but so often, I fell short. One day I prayed, "Dear Lord, I am really frustrated by my many failures. I don't think I even have any hope to be corrected by Your precepts. What shall I do?"

As I was praying with a feeling of despair, the Holy Spirit began to speak in my heart.

Sunja, you must know that it is impossible for you to be a perfectly righteous person in My sight, as Scripture says, "For all have sinned and fall short of the glory of God, and are justified freely by his grace through the redemption that came by Christ Jesus" (Romans 3:23-24). Because of your falling short of the glory of God, My Son died for you. If you are perfectly righteous to enter the Kingdom of Heaven, why was My Son crucified as a sacrificial lamb? It is because your good deeds are still not good enough to save you. Therefore, whenever you discover your sins, you must give thanks to My Son, Jesus, who became your justification.

So never forget that Jesus Christ is the only way to heaven, not your own righteousness. In other words, Jesus became a bridge that connects God and humans through the shedding of His precious blood. Yet, through Christ, you should still keep growing in godly character for the sake of God's glory. You should be a light in this dark world.

In this way, my wonderful counselor, the Holy Spirit, completely released me from my guilty burden. God's peace came into my heart again!

The third story is prefaced by the fact that I had been popular since junior high because of my sense of humor. My older and younger brothers were very funny, and I learned from them. My classmates loved my humorous expression, and I was a popular student until I graduated from college. This gave me great pride.

However, after my rebirth, whenever I prayed to God, I felt uneasy about my daily jokes and secular conversations. I repented day after day regarding my frivolous words and shallow conversations. Gradually, I changed little by little, and I became quieter instead of my normal chatty self. Making progress was slow. It took almost a year of repenting for my continued mistakes. One day, while I was struggling, the Holy Spirit spoke to me: "If you are always joking around, the words of Jesus Christ from your mouth will be considered a joke as well." Soon after I improved in this area, I realized the power of the Holy Spirit accompanying me whenever I talked about the gospel. Later, I shared the gospel with two fellow professors, and they became believers. Another one with whom I shared the gospel is still searching for Christ, but she sent me a letter when I was living in Texas in which she wrote, "Watching your amazing transformation made me believe in God's existence." Fast forward to over forty years later, I found out in 2019 that she had been baptized a few months earlier.

> But among you there must not be even a hint of sexual immorality, or of any kind of impurity, or of greed, because these are improper for God's holy people. Nor should there be obscenity, foolish talk or coarse joking, which are out of place, but rather thanksgiving. (Ephesians 5:3-4)

The final story happened when I was an assistant teacher. I feared the chief professor because she had the power to fire or promote me. When she sometimes got angry with me, I became fearful of the consequences because I had wanted to be promoted to a professorship for a long time. One day, I was one hour late to school, and my boss got very angry and severely scolded me.

At home after work, I was worried about this matter until the Holy Spirit spoke to me.

> Don't fear people; fear God only, for I set before you life and prosperity, death and destruction. Blessings and curses belong to Me.

Through these lessons, I clearly learned that only God has the power of life and death and to give prosperity or destruction. Whenever I face tribulations, I bring them to God. "Come to me, all you who are weary and burdened, and I will give you rest" (Matthew 11:28).

7

THE BUS FARE GOD GAVE ME

It was March of 1973. I had to go up to Seoul before leaving my country for America. All citizens who go abroad must receive anti-communism education as a legal policy of the government. So I went to my parents' house in Seoul from Taegu, where I was living with my oldest son, who was two years old. The next morning, as I was about to leave my home, my best friend called and asked me to stop by her house for lunch. After the class, I was waiting for the bus to go to my friend's house with my son. The bus didn't come for a while, so I looked around and saw a store selling children's clothing just behind me. I walked in to buy better clothes for my son before seeing my friend's family. I spent all the money I had with me except for what I'd need for the return bus fare. I thought that I had enough money in my suitcase for the next day's trip to Taegu. When I got back to my parents' house after visiting my friend, I checked to see how much money I had left. I was short ten cents for the bus fare I needed to return. This would be a small problem for most people, but it was a really big issue for me. I had given my born-again testimony to my family before, so they imagined that I would be able to live like the angels. They also thought that I could manage my life perfectly. I wanted to be a good example to them not only for the glory of God but also for their spiritual new birth. This money shortage was caused by my own reckless deed.

I was a grown-up who had a professional job and had lived independently for a long time. How could I ask my parents for ten cents? It would seem ridiculous to them. I knelt down and prayed, "Father, I spent my money carelessly this afternoon. Please forgive my foolish act. I urgently need ten cents for the bus fare to get home from the Taegu station. I can't walk such a long distance with a two-year-old boy, and also I must go to my coworker's wedding at two o'clock tomorrow afternoon, so I don't have time to walk home. Dear Father, I really need Your help. Please grant my petition. Otherwise, I will be in big trouble. Please give me ten cents. I pray this in Jesus' name, amen." I repeated the same prayer more than ten times because I wasn't sure if God had heard me. It was a big dilemma for me, and I was anxious all night long. While I was praying, I imagined that God would have my parents give me some money to buy my son's snack for the bus ride, which takes four hours. The next morning, as soon as I woke up, I prayed again, "Dear God, my hope is only in You. If You don't accept my petition, I will be in extreme distress. Please, help my problem." I prayed this over and over again as I did the night before. I believed God would have finally heard my ardent prayers. Afterward, I ate breakfast with my parents. Then it was time to leave, so I took my luggage. The time came where I anticipated my father giving me some money, but nothing happened. No offer of money! Why wasn't God answering my prayers? Why was He not listening? I was so disturbed to face this unexpected situation. I didn't know what to do. I tried to take my time in order to give myself more of a chance to get some money from my parents. Despite my strategy, they didn't give me any money.

As I left my parents' house with a feeling of desperation, the strong March wind shut the gate behind me as I heard my parents say a final goodbye. I was stunned by God's silence. I wondered if I should go back and ask them for ten cents. But I stopped myself from doing that because I knew how disgraceful it would be. I would rather give up than go back. After I stood for a while in the windy weather, I was compelled to leave with a feeling of utter hopelessness.

I went to the bus stop nearby to go to the long-distance bus station. The total amount I had was $100, plus another $1.10 in coins. I paid a quarter for the bus fare to get to the station from my parents' house and had $100.85 remaining. The bus fare to Taegu was $100.70, leaving me with fifteen cents, but I still needed ten cents to pay the local bus fare—a quarter—to get home. I prayed without ceasing while riding to the Seoul bus station. I got off the bus in front of the station. Then I went in and got in line to buy a ticket. There were several people ahead of me, but no one was behind me. At last, the person in front of me was buying her ticket at the selling window, with no one behind me still. At that exact moment, a young man approached me and asked, "Are you going to Taegu?" I said, "Yes, I am." He smiled at me and then asked, "Would you like to buy my ticket? My friends want me to stay in Seoul one more day." There were a few young men around him. I told him, "Of course. I can buy your ticket, no problem!" I received his ticket and gave him $100 right away. Then I had to count out the seventy cents from the eighty-five cents I had left with. While I was counting out the change, he was still standing by me to receive it. Then suddenly he shouted, "Lady, it's okay, I have to go now." I told him, "Wait a minute, I'll give you the change." After I finished counting, I lifted my head, but I didn't see him. I looked around to find him, but he was nowhere to be found. He completely disappeared. I looked down, and I had the full seventy cents in my hand, for a grand total of eighty-five cents! That small amount of change seemed like a million dollars at that moment. My God! He performed the miracle for my desperate need. I asked Him only for ten cents, but He gave me seventy cents! I jumped and jumped with overwhelming joy and went out of the station. I bought a big piece of bread for my son's lunch and a package of gum that he liked with the extra money God had generously given me. I was even able to treat the woman sitting next to me with a piece of gum. How awesome is God! He had planned perfectly for my prayer in advance. I have never forgotten this amazing event.

As I reflect on this, I realize that my prayer was answered not by my idea but by God's plan. My idea was that God would answer my prayer for the bus fare by moving my parents to give me money like they had in the past. If this had happened, I would not have remembered this story so many years later like I do now. But it was God's way—through a stranger and at the last second—that showed me His thoughts are the best and made this story so memorable. The Scripture says, "'For my thoughts are not your thoughts, neither are your ways my ways,' declares the LORD. 'As the heavens are higher than the earth, so are my ways higher than your ways and my thoughts than your thoughts'" (Isaiah 55:8-9). The young man selling his bus ticket had no other option except me when he came to the station. God planned all these happenings perfectly for my need. In short, God put me in the proper place at the proper time for the proper person. My eternal Father solved my petition by His incredibly perfect plan, which transcended all my understanding in impossible ways that humans could not imagine. I am so extremely joyful that I can live in the presence of almighty God on my road of life. Proverbs 16:9 reminds us that "in his heart a man plans his course, but the LORD determines his steps." He also reminds us in Psalms that "the LORD is near to all who call on him, to all who call on him in truth. He fulfills the desires of those who fear him; he hears their cry and saves them" (Psalm 145:18-19).

Finally, God says to us in the book of Jeremiah, "'For I know the plans I have for you,' declares the LORD, 'plans to prosper you and not to harm you, plans to give you hope and a future. Then you will call upon me and come and pray to me, and I will listen to you. You will seek me and find me when you seek me with all your heart'" (Jeremiah 29:11-13).

8
HOW MY HEAVENLY FATHER PROVIDED ME
MY BELOVED KIMCHI

It was August of 1975. Right after my husband finished graduate school, he got admitted to the University of California in Berkeley for his PhD. We packed what little belongings we owned into our old, beat-up Chevrolet that we had purchased for $400 and headed out for the long drive through west Texas to California. It was really hot as we drove through the stifling heat of a Texas summer, and we used the only air conditioner our car had—rolled-down windows.

As we were about to leave Austin, one Korean foreign student generously gave us a medium-sized bag of rice. It was a very thoughtful gift because I hadn't been able to prepare in advance for our travel as there were too many things to do. At this time we had a four-month-old baby and a four-year-old boy. While we were heading toward El Paso, our old 1960 Chevrolet began to have trouble, and oil started leaking from the engine. We went to a gas station, but they couldn't fix it. We prayed to God for help. After a while, we found a car repair shop. They temporarily blocked the leaking hole with a special solution. As it was getting dark, we decided to stay at a Motel 6, where I cooked the rice in our electric rice cooker. We needed some spicy side dishes like kimchi or hot pepper paste that are always eaten with plain cooked rice, but one couldn't find any of these familiar spicy foods at the grocery stores in west Texas in the 1970s. I ended up buying a jar of cucumber pickles and a can of tuna. We didn't enjoy the meal at all because we missed the spicy side dishes.

The next day I cooked rice again, but it was so painful to eat without kimchi or hot paste. Whenever we ate the rice, we missed the Korean spicy dishes, especially kimchi. After three days, we arrived in El Paso. We booked a room at a Motel 6. After we put some of our belongings in our motel room, we went to the grocery store to buy a few things we needed. There were a few small grocery stores in close proximity to where we were staying, and we randomly chose one.

When my husband was paying for our groceries, I saw two Asian adults who seemed to be a couple standing in front of the checkout line. It was so exciting for me to meet Asians because so few lived in that area at that time. I was wondering if they were Korean. After my husband paid for our things, I shyly approached them and asked where they were from. To my delight, they said they were from Korea and shared with me that they were waiting for us until we finished paying. We were all pleased to see each other. They were a married couple, and the husband was studying as a foreign student at the University of Texas at El Paso. As we were chatting and walking to the parking lot, they invited us to their apartment house, telling us it was very small. At that time, most Korean foreign students were poor like us.

We arrived at their small apartment. As soon as we entered the house, I saw something that piqued my interest. There were three small jars of kimchi on a shelf by the window. It was a glorious sight. Without any hesitation, I exclaimed loudly, "Ah! Kimchi!" I was surprised by my outburst as the couple smiled at me. During our time in Texas, the ingredients that make up kimchi, such as Napa cabbage and Korean red pepper powder, could rarely be found in any of the Texas grocery stores. While we were chatting, the wife told us with embarrassment that they only had kimchi and rice and no other side dishes. She asked if we would be okay with that. I exclaimed, "That sounds amazing!" I was so happy to hear their offer. I was thanking God from the bottom of my heart. My heavenly Father knew how much I had been longing for kimchi for the previous three days. My husband and I ate only rice and kimchi that night, but it felt like the most delicious three-star Michelin rated restaurant in the world. Up to that point in my life, it was the best meal I ever had.

After we happily enjoyed their mouth-watering meal, I thanked them profusely. And then I told them that we had to leave. As we were getting ready to depart, I was desperately hoping that they might offer us just one jar of kimchi for the rest of our trip, but there was no way I could ask them for it because in our culture that would be rude. At last, we stood up to leave. I heard the husband whispering something to his wife, but I could hardly hear him. I hoped that it was a conversation about the kimchi. Soon after, the wife said to us, "Would you like to take a jar of kimchi with you for your trip?" I couldn't even hide my joyful astonishment. My wish had come true! I hadn't even prayed to God for the kimchi, yet my heavenly Father knew my craving for it. We thanked them profusely again and happily left Texas for California—with a jar of kimchi through the love of God.

9
THE STORY OF MY HUSBAND

I had been dating my fiancée for two years before I was born again. We were supposed to marry in April of 1969. My conversion happened two months prior, in February of 1969. When I was simply a church attendee, I was open to the idea of marrying a non-believer. Sometimes I would ask him to go to church with me, but he would say, "I'll go later." I tried to make him a churchgoer, but after being born again, I knew I couldn't marry him. Spiritually, he was a dead person. There was no life in him in the sight of God, but I had become a living soul and had God's eternal life. The purpose of my life had changed for God's Kingdom. How could I marry someone whose spirit was dead? I couldn't marry someone who did not share my deepest value—to live for Christ.

As I was walking home after our first date since I had become a believer, I prayed to God,

> Dear Father, before I encountered the living God, I was willing to
> marry a non-believer. I even promised him that I would marry him,
> but now that I have experienced You, I can't marry him.

He had spent a considerable amount of time and money while he dated me, and he truly loved me. The thought of breaking up with him was very difficult, and so I prayed,

> Father, if You think this man can't be my future husband, please
> help us to break up in Your grace, without any pain. But if You think
> this man could be my husband, please let him become Your son. I
> will share with him the gospel from this day forward. I pray this in
> Jesus' name, amen.

From that moment, I began to share with him about how someone can be born again of the Holy Spirit. Surprisingly, he had believed God's existence already through a near-death experience, but the journey to Christ still had to take place. Here is his testimony in his own words:

Self-Reliance

A wise son heeds his father's instruction, but a mocker does not listen to rebuke. (Proverbs 13:1)

This message teaches us to confess our sins and humble ourselves to God's Word. However, when I was younger, I considered myself a bright, intelligent, self-made man. At the age of 27, however, I found myself in a dark illusion of arrogance and sin. There were good reasons for the sin of my ignorance. I was an academic overachiever. I was always top ranked in my class from elementary to high school except in the first grade. I was the first runner up in a province-wide entrance exam for middle school in South Korea. I went to the top high school in the province, and the list of academic achievements goes on: I was an academic celebrity in my hometown, was among the top high school graduates, and was pursued by numerous colleges and universities. A local college offered me a full scholarship for four years, but I proudly declined this offer because I was accepted to Seoul National University, the dream college for all Koreans!

I was proud of myself for being one of the "geniuses" in Korea. I became an enviable engineering student at Seoul National University. I was particularly proud because my achievement was the sole product of my talent and capability without financial support from my parents. Though I came from a humble rural village, I was the cream of the crop. My parents were poor peasants and barely earned enough for daily bread. I had to rely on my independence, self-confidence, and intellect to fulfill my ambitions. My goal was to become a big-name scientist who would be known around the world. I was ambitious and intelligent, but I was also arrogant and a non-believer. Religion was not an option for me because I felt it was useless under the power of science.

Despair

I learned the uselessness of human versions of knowledge and ambitions in a painful way. It started in the winter of my eighth-grade year. My loving father passed away after a long struggle with illness. His death left a huge emptiness and many questions. What is the purpose of life? Why should people die? Where do we go after death? As I said previously, I was an assertive, outgoing, and self-confident youth. But these unanswered questions slowly began to transform my character into a withdrawn, skeptical, and aimless boy. Our family's poverty worsened after the death of my father. My college life was nothing but a struggle. It could have been easier if I had accepted the scholarship from the local university near my hometown. However, I chose Seoul National University, without a scholarship, to guarantee lifelong benefits as a graduate from the top university in Korea.

Moreover, my pride, or more likely arrogance, did not permit me to attend a humble third-tier school at that time. My financial destitution reached its zenith during my college years. I worked as a private tutor, but it did not earn enough to cover my college tuition and living expenses. I often had to walk for several miles between the dormitory and workplace because I was not able to pay for public transportation. I had to survive for days without food on numerous occasions. Skepticism and hopelessness became the dominant theme of my life. I indulged in Schopenhauer and Nietzsche and had impulsive desires to follow a railroad track that would lead to potential death.

The worst came at the end of my college years. I was a candidate to become a Korean Army officer under the ROTC program, but after two years of training, doctors found tuberculosis in my lungs during a physical examination. It was probably caused by malnutrition, chronic fatigue from overworking, and bone-crushing military training. As a result, I was disqualified from being a Korean Army officer. I blamed this on the poverty and death of my father. Full of disappointment, despair, and hopelessness, my life had truly hit rock bottom.

I moved down to a provincial city near my hometown, got a dismal job, and began to nurse my lungs. However, my lungs did not get better even after three years of intense medication. Instead, the medication weakened my stomach. My doctor said that the hole in my lung grew to about an inch in diameter, and surgical removal of the infected lung was the only way to save my life. Without surgery, I was not likely to live more than three months. It was a death sentence for me, but I was not capable of financing the cost of this surgery. Korea was not a rich country in the 1960s, and there was no insurance or welfare for medical coverage. My mother opposed the surgery because she did not want me to live a miserable life without functional lungs, and no one in my family could cover the cost. I took her opposition as betrayal. The only option for me was to die. I moved to my sister's house in a remote rural village and waited for death. I plunged deeply into a "valley of the shadow of death."

Surrendering to Jesus Christ

I grew up in poverty without a father. I never trusted anyone but myself. I believed that I was the only one who could plan and live my life. I had to build my self-confidence and will to live. An arrogant ego dominated my soul. However, everything of my own was powerless against this imminent death. The fear of death put cracks in the wall of my ego. Beyond the horizon of death, the rays of God's love began to reach me through the fissures. As I awaited death, I did nothing but wander aimlessly along roads or sit and lie down under trees outside of my sister's rural home. On one of those days, a melody of church bells tapped my ears. The bell had likely rung countless times before, but I never heard it in the way I did at that moment. It was different. It caused my heart to pound. The bells came into me and calmed my fears a little bit, and I felt a sense of peace. The three months my doctor predicted I had to live had passed, but I was still alive. Curious and puzzled, I consulted with a doctor of oriental medicine who was a distant relative of mine. He suggested a re-examination because he suspected my illness was something other than tuberculosis. I took the exam at a local hospital, and it turned out to be a lung fluke, a type of parasite, and not tuberculosis. I was prescribed medication for it, and within a month I was completely cured! I could have been furious about the misdiagnosis because four years of my life seemed wasted with excruciating agonies, distress, and struggles. Nowadays in the United States, this would have been compelling grounds for malpractice and litigation, but I did not want to blame anyone because I was so grateful for the second opportunity at new life. It was a life after death that was given to me by God. God began to replace my arrogance, ego, and all my own efforts with His love. I thanked God for the poverty of my family because it prevented the surgery, thereby saving my lungs, and I particularly thanked my mother. The Lord ultimately provided me with poverty to prepare a new life to live for Him. It was a blessed gift from God!

I went to a Catholic church, not a Protestant one, for several months. There were a couple of reasons for this: First, I liked the quiet and holy environment of the Catholic church. Second, I did not have a good impression of Protestants because I saw a lot of conflicts, disputes, and divisions in the Protestant churches in Korea. I thought all Protestants were hypocrites. I tried to learn the Bible from a well-known priest, but our study sessions did not give me answers to my fundamental questions: Who is Jesus Christ? Who am I? Why should people die? Soon, I left the Catholic church. Meanwhile, I met the most important woman in my life. She was raised in a sincere Protestant Christian family. She asked me to go to her church, but I was reluctant to do so due to my biased impression of Protestants. She gave me a Bible, but I did not read it. However, she never quit trying to persuade me. Finally, I agreed to attend a Bible class in English that was taught by an American missionary at the local YMCA. To be honest, I was more interested in learning English than I was in the Bible. The first class was interesting and pleasant, particularly the gospel songs and Bible stories. Its open hospitality appeased my negative attitude toward Protestants. But most importantly, I opened the Bible for the first time in my life!

In February 1969, I witnessed a dramatic change in my fiancée. She was no longer the lady whom I had previously known. She was a brand-new person. I saw ecstatic illuminations in her face. She was like an angel. She testified, full of joy, that she was reborn by the power of the Savior, Jesus Christ. From that point on, our conversations were only centered on Jesus. She gave me lucid answers to my life-long questions that were based on the Bible. (1) I am a sinner; this was the answer to my question "Who am I?" (2) We all die because the wages of sin is death—the answer to the question "Why do we die?" (3) We will stand in the Court of God for final judgment, for this is the destination after death. These were very simple answers that I pursued during my life of confusion and struggle. "I am a sinner and will be judged by God after death." These answers were readily acceptable to me because of my near-death experience. I knelt down in front of Jesus Christ. I wanted to put my life of sin in the past for a new life ahead with Jesus Christ. I repented, "My Lord, I am a sinner!" Soon I saw the sin of my body in a picture of my soul. I saw the dark pathogens of sin in my skin, chest, abdomen, and everywhere else. The Lord always looks into our souls and not at our external appearances. Our knowledge, philanthropy, discipline, and all other human subjects are the externals, and they cannot erase our sins against God. "If we claim to be without sin, we deceive ourselves and the truth is not in us. If we confess our sins, he is faithful and just and will forgive us our sins and purify us from all unrighteousness. If we claim we have not sinned, we make him out to be a liar and his word has no place in our lives" (1 John 1:8-10). We are all sinners to God, so I continued my prayer and pledged to the Lord, "Jesus Christ, my Savior, please allow me to have a new life. Please cleanse my sins with Your holy blood." This prayer shifted my entire life only to the Lord.

Life after Rebirth

John the Baptist said of Jesus Christ, "Look, the Lamb of God, who takes away the sin of the world! This is the one I meant when I said, 'A man who comes after me has surpassed me because he was before me'" (John 1:29-30). My ego and arrogance were demolished after surrendering myself to the Lord. The Lord replaced my knowledge and pride with His blessed faith. I began on my pilgrimage path to God after twenty-seven years of aimless drifting. I submitted myself to Jesus Christ and ceased all activities that did not comply with Him. I became a regular attendee of church instead of the pubs and bars I had previously frequented. The blessing of His message often made me become emotional during the sermons. The love of God warmed and softened my cold and hardened heart. It drew a clear picture of the true love of Jesus Christ, who bled and died for us. He sacrificed His own life for sinners like me. Thanks and praise to Him alone! My friends were curious about my change because it was so different from my previous way of life.

A few months later, I came back to Seoul because I was offered a position by the prestigious Korean Institute of Science and Technology. This was a dream career for all Korean scientists and engineers. However, I had to face another roadblock. My employer found my old record of tuberculosis and denied medical clearance for my employment. I explained to my employer the tuberculosis was a misdiagnosis. They ordered me to take another physical examination at a credible medical institution. I became anxious and nervous again. "What if indeed it was tuberculosis? Should I repeat the punishing ordeal that I went through?" I took an X-ray at the Seoul National University hospital and waited for the verdict from a lung specialist. My name was called, and I went into his office. My heart pounded like blasting missiles. I couldn't even take a single breath. He looked at my chart and said, "Who the hell said you had tuberculosis? You would be a dead man already if it were tuberculosis." Hallelujah! My medical record was cleared! In the cab on the way back, I burst into tears. Yes, I was indeed a dead man and reborn with the Lord! Praise Him! I also saw the tears falling from the sky outside the car window: It was rain from Him.

A Dream from God

I cannot forget a dream that I had after accepting Jesus Christ as my Savior. In this dream, I was laid on a bed in a hospital operating room. A few doctors tried to operate on me by removing my lungs, but they soon gave up and left the operating room saying to each other, "This guy is hopeless." I was alone, lying on the operating table. A piece of bread floated in the air above my face. It was like a jewel, brightly illuminated from a pure white object. It descended down into my mouth. I ate it, and then I heard a vivid voice: "I cured you perfectly, so surrender to Me." The Lord showed me a clear path for my life. My life would now be for Him, not for myself. I kept praying. A feeling of true and perfect peace came down into my soul. Since then, I have never been anxious, nervous, or doubtful about my lungs. I became confident with my career and life within Jesus Christ, not myself. He cured my body and saved my soul for a new life in His way. To end this testimony, my gratitude and praise to Him can be summed up in these verses: "The LORD is my shepherd, I shall not be in want. He makes me lie down in green pastures, he leads me beside quiet waters, he restores my soul. He guides me in paths of righteousness for his name's sake" (Psalm 23:1-3).

This was my husband's testimony. My husband was a brilliant scientist and was a pioneer in the field of nanofluid mechanics.

10

THE WISDOM GOD GAVE ME FOR MY UNEASY MARRIAGE

My husband and I were married on October 20, 1969, on a beautiful fall day soon after my husband accepted Jesus Christ as his Savior. We went on our honeymoon, and as soon as we got into the hotel room, I suggested having a prayer time for our successful and happy married life for the glory of God. As we knelt down and prayed together, I felt that my heart was being touched by the Holy Spirit and perceived that God would greatly bless our marriage. But to my surprise, my newlywed life was unhappy for me as I began to notice my husband's weaknesses. Sometimes he seemed to act like a child and spoke unreasonably. Instead of living the happy newlywed life, my heart began to be troubled. Over time, I couldn't respect him and accept him as he was. He irritated me in many ways, and I felt no love toward him. My sweet dreams of marriage were shattered. I was devastated and unsure of what I should do.

I had married him in the sight of God with the minister officiating it. I couldn't divorce him because I had vowed "until death do us part" before the living God. I was so distressed that I knelt down to pray, "Dear heavenly Father, what am I supposed to do? I really need Your help." My prayer continued day after day. About two months after I started praying this prayer, I went to the church for a Sunday worship service. The topic of the sermon was the meaning of Christian marriage. The pastor shared this illustration:

> A farmer was scattering seeds far over the fields. Another man who was in the distance saw this farmer and thought that there was just the one farmer sowing. But as he drew closer, he found that there were two people there: One was a leper who had no hands but had feet. On his back was a leper who had no feet but had hands. So they became one body, which made their task possible.

46

The minister said that this story was designed to illustrate the Word of God concerning how a couple should live. In Genesis 2:20 it says, "For Adam no suitable helper was found." I was astonished that God would so clearly answer my prayer through the sermon. I realized that I had been thinking of my husband as a perfect leper who had two hands and two feet, so I had expected him to be a perfect and ideal helper. That's why I was so frustrated and unhappy with him.

God taught me that a husband has 50% strengths and 50% weaknesses and that we were brought together to complement each other's strengths and weaknesses. Thus, together, we could become one whole body, 50% plus 50%. I began to consider our differences. We were opposite in various aspects. For example, while I had many friends and was extroverted, he had only a few and was introverted. He was good at organization, but I was not. I was a frugal person, but he was not. And on and on the list of strengths and weaknesses went. Where I was strong, he was often weak. Where he was strong, I was weak. I realized we really were like those two lepers. Alone, we would not be enough for our journey, but if we complemented each other, we could take on life's challenges together.

This was just the first of many lessons the Holy Spirit would teach me. The Monday after that Sunday service, I had to go to work, which was located on the outskirts of the city. There were two kinds of buses bound for the university at the bus stop near my house. One was a shorter route to get there, so I always took this bus route. On that particular day, I got on the bus and realized that for the first time ever, I had taken the wrong bus. This route ended up taking thirty minutes longer to reach my destination. It was a huge mistake as it was a very busy morning for me at work.

My uneasiness was growing as I looked outside the bus window. The spring sun was shining so beautifully. Meanwhile, I saw one scene of an aged couple who were working together in their small farmyard. As the old husband was making furrows, the wife was following behind her husband scattering seeds along the furrows. the scene illustrated a loving and peaceful relationship of an elderly couple. I believe God led me to view this beautiful scene. Before, I had an idea that my husband should do both plowing and planting. Although I had been thinking in a self-centered way, I hadn't realized I was a very selfish and silly person. I expected to be treated like a princess by my husband, who had promised this life to me when we were dating. Through the affectionate old couple, I came to realize that the meaning of marriage should be to help and serve one another and work together without criticizing each other. In this way, my perspective on marriage changed, and I tried to accept my husband as he was and fill up his weak points. But the path of my marriage was still not smooth.

11
HOW GOD LED ME AWAY FROM DIVORCE

I continued to have a difficult time with my husband while he was studying as a PhD student at the University of California in Berkeley. I was working as a babysitter for two children at my home along with watching my own young boys. One day, my husband came home earlier than usual. He always wanted the house to be clean, so I used to tidy up before he came home every evening. But that day, I wasn't aware that he would come home so early. He was livid because of the slightly messy house. The anxiety and stress caused me to go into the children's room, and I prayed to God in tears, "Dear Father, I can't continue to live with a critical husband any longer. Lord, You know his anger often lasts exceptionally long over small incidents, so it has given me high stress. Father, if I divorce him, won't it help him to realize that he has treated the children and me so harshly? I hope he will one day repent of this. Of course, I don't want a divorce, but if divorce would help him realize his wrong behavior, I will do it. If You don't want me to divorce him, I won't. *Please let me know what Your will is.* I pray this in Jesus' name, amen."

After a while, I fell asleep and had a dream. I was sick. My older sister and my favorite aunt came to help me. They laid me on a light bed, and I flew in the air while they were holding my bed. It wasn't long before we landed in a town. We went into a big house, and there was a large amount of fresh beef on the dining table in the hall. I said to my sister, "I'm hungry. Let's cook the beef and eat and then fly again."

As soon as I finished talking, a strange man came from the other side and said, "I'll cook for you." After he cooked the meat, we ate his delicious meal and went into the backyard. I saw two big bathrooms on the right side. I went toward the bathrooms and spit at them. I said, "Older sister, usually there are filthy things around the backyard of most houses." As soon as I was done spitting and speaking, one of the bathroom's doors opened with a crash, and the image of Satan, like what you would see in a children's cartoon, appeared before us. The devil pointed at my heart with his right finger and said three times in English (not my native Korean), "You should be divorced! You should be divorced! You should be divorced!" I was so scared in my dream and woke up feeling terrified. I couldn't stay in the room because of the horrifying dream. I felt there was still a dark presence in the room, so I ran to the room where my husband slept and discovered the door was open. When I saw my husband sleeping, my fear was lessened. I leaned against the door frame, and talked to my heavenly Father, "Oh, God! I realize now, through the dream, that Satan wants us to divorce. I now know that the desire of the evil spirit is to keep our family from being a godly witness to the world by pushing me toward divorce. Thank You for answering my prayer and showing me what Your good will is for my marriage."

Afterward, I laid down by my husband and told him, "Let's not get tempted by the evil spirit." I was almost completely unaware of what I was saying. Later, my husband told me that he felt dread when he heard my words. My good Father had kept my uneasy marriage from the hand of Satan's attack.

"Haven't you read," [Jesus] replied, "that at the beginning the Creator 'made them male and female,' and said, 'For this reason a man will leave his father and mother and be united to his wife, and the two will become one flesh'? So they are no longer two, but one. Therefore what God has joined together, let man not separate." (Matthew 19:4-6)

12
LEARNING ABOUT FORGIVENESS

Our family was scheduled to go on a vacation with some church friends, including the pastor's family, for four days in Lake Tahoe, California. We were supposed to meet at the pastor's house at ten o'clock in the morning. I woke up early to prepare everything on time, but there were too many things to do. I had to make breakfast, wash the dishes, clean up the kitchen area, put clothes on my two-year-old son, and pack enough clothes and groceries for four days. After all the work, I had to put on makeup and do my hair, too. I felt very overwhelmed without any help from my husband. He was just sitting on the chair and waiting for us to get ready to leave. It was about time to go, but I wasn't quite ready. I was really afraid to anger him because he was punctual to the minute.

Finally, everything was ready to go, but I was about ten minutes late. Thankfully, my husband did not get angry. He helped me put everything into the car and began to drive to the pastor's home. After about ten minutes of driving, he started yelling at me for being late. I wanted to say, "Don't blame it on me only. You didn't help me at all!" Instead, I chose to keep quiet because I knew it would only make matters worse if I talked back. At one point, he parked on the side of the road and kept scolding me. I was afraid that he was going to go back home because sometimes he would do that if we were late. After a while, thankfully, he started driving to the pastor's house again. When we arrived, the pastor and his family were not even packed yet. The family room and kitchen were still messy with things they were going to bring on the trip.

Even so, the pastor was gentle, kind, and helpful to his wife. I began to feel angry as I compared my husband's attitude to the pastor's. We waited for nearly an hour for them to be ready. On the three-hour drive to Lake Tahoe, I didn't say one word to my husband because of my anger. After we arrived,

I went to the lake to be alone and talked to God. I was feeling angry and hurt. "Dear God, could I stay married to this critical, cold man for the rest of my life? And also, whenever he shouts at me, how much does it hurt my little sons, whom I love so deeply? Father, I am very sad not just for myself but especially for my two sons." As I continued to pray, the Lord began to speak to me, "Recite the Lord's prayer carefully in its exact order." I had memorized it during Sunday school. I knew the words well, but I had never paid attention to what it meant. So I slowly began to recite it with deep concentration, seeking God's answer. "Our Father in heaven, hallowed be Your name, Your Kingdom come, Your will be done, on earth as it is in heaven. Give us today our daily bread. Forgive us our sins, as we also have forgiven our neighbor's sins." When I reached the part of the prayer about forgiving our sins as we have forgiven our neighbor's sins, I perceived the meaning of these words for the first time in my Christian life. God's Spirit continually asked me, "Have you not sinned in My sight?" My reply was, "Of course, God. I have sinned many times in Your sight." God responded, "Right! So if you want Me to forgive your sins, what do you have to do first?" I said, "I must forgive my neighbor's sins first." God spoke, "Yes, you are right."

At that time, for the first time, I realized that my husband was one of my neighbors. In the past, I did not count my husband as a neighbor but only as my husband. God asked me again, "Don't you think you could commit some sins in your future?" I replied, "Oh, God! Of course I will do that." God said, "Then always forgive your neighbor's sins, and then ask for My forgiveness for your own sins." I remarked, "Okay, Father, I will forgive my husband with delight. And I'll forgive all my other neighbor's sins as well." I was so happy that I could learn this valuable lesson from my perfect Counselor, my Creator. I came back to the retreat house with great pleasure and kindly conversed with my husband.

Since that precious dialogue with God, it has become easier for me to offer forgiveness to my neighbors, including my husband. Whenever my husband spoke to me in anger, I recalled God's counsel at Lake Tahoe. Thank God always! God gave me a prescription of forgiveness to lift my burdens away.

13
MELTING THE ICE

In August of 1975, our young family moved from Austin, Texas, to Berkeley, California. One fall evening, I went to a parents' meeting for my four-year-old son's preschool. My husband was taking care of our two little boys. When I came back home from the meeting, the older son said to me, "Mommy, Daddy spanked David because he was crying." When I heard his words, my heart was torn apart by my husband's unreasonable behavior. I thought he showed a lack of common sense. How in the world could he spank my second son as he was only a baby? My infant son had a very gentle disposition that had caused no trouble. I was so dismayed by my husband's heartless action. I appealed to the Lord with a broken heart, "Dear Father, I can't understand his behavior at all. I'm in deep sorrow and compassion for my two little boys who are growing up under such a heartless father." I was weeping quietly in the other room. Suddenly, I recognized God's tender and quiet voice speaking to my spirit. He called me by my name, "Sunja, there is a block of ice here. If another block of ice is in contact with it, what will happen?" I responded, "Nothing will happen. The ice will remain as it is." God said, "Correct. Then if a block of ice needs to be melted away, what needs to happen?" I said, "Heat should be directed toward it." God explained, "Exactly, the fire of love is the heat that should go toward it. Right now, both of your hearts are like blocks of ice." God revealed that my husband's hard heart could be melted by the fire of love through me. Since that time, I tried to love my husband unconditionally, but my love seemed so limited that it was impossible for me to express the fire of love. So I asked God to fill me up with His limitless love so that I could live according to God's will. Without the help of the Holy Spirit, I realized that it is impossible to give God's love to my neighbors. That's the reason why Jesus Christ, the son of God, laid down His life on the cross for our redemption and for our falling short of the glory of God. Without His redemption, no one could come to the Kingdom of God.

> This is love: not that we loved God, but that he loved us and sent his Son as an atoning sacrifice for our sins. Dear friends, since God so loved us, we also ought to love one another. (1 John 4:10-11)

14
MY HUSBAND'S TRANSFORMATION

As time went by, my husband and I had been changing little by little toward God's measureless love. But I still had some difficulty with him. By the age of fifty-five, my husband had changed the way he parented. He was kinder to his four sons, and his growth made me very happy. But he was still critical with me.

Around 2011, my husband was sick on occasion though he had been in good health for a long time. He would become dizzy and his back began to burn with pain, but his physician told him there were no problems. He advised him to take some Advil for his back pain. In early October of 2011, my husband made an appointment with a chiropractor for his agonizing back pain. At the time, it hurt him simply to take one step. The chiropractor strongly urged him to get an X-ray for his severe back pain. The X-ray lit up with three cancerous tumors that were squeezing into his spinal cord. One of my sons took him to the emergency room at Northwestern hospital in downtown Chicago.

After taking a CT scan, the specialist came in with devastating news: my husband had late-stage prostate cancer that had spread throughout his bones. His spine was filled with tumors that were so large they were squeezing his spinal cord. The radiation oncologist urged immediate radiation on his back because the tumors could snap his spinal cord at any moment. With the help of emergency radiation treatments and hormone therapy, my husband would live for fourteen more months.

During his fight with cancer, my husband became a very gentle person. He never complained about his severe pain. It felt like I was married to an angel. He cooked food with or without me; before this, he would never cook. He no longer got angry with me. Before every breakfast, he would read some words from the Bible, and we would pray together. One morning, my husband read from 1 Corinthians 13:4-5, "Love is patient, love is kind. It does not envy, it does not boast, it is not proud. It is not rude, it is not self-seeking, it is not easily angered."

At this point, he paused from his reading, turned to me, and apologized for not being loving enough, especially for getting angry so easily over the many years. His humble apology melted my heart. My God had finally made him an ideal husband, even though the happiness was only for a very short time. He passed away in January of 2013 at the age of 71 in the hope of the resurrection.

My oldest son gave a eulogy for his late father. In it, he said, "'There's a land that is fairer than day. And by faith we can see it afar. For the Father waits over the way, to prepare us a dwelling place there.' Goodbye, Abba (Dad in Korean). We shall meet you on that beautiful shore."

After my husband left us, I repented deeply in tears for my lack of love and understanding toward him while he was with me in this temporary world. I should have loved him more like God had wanted me to do. In this situation, God clearly taught me that I have to build up all human relationships on the foundation of His love and forgiveness. The Bible teaches us that our relationship with God is first and our relationship with our neighbors is second. "'Love the Lord your God with all your heart and with all your soul and with all your mind.' This is the first and greatest commandment. And the second is like it: 'Love your neighbor as yourself'" (Matthew 22:37-39).

Although I truly wanted to give my husband the deep love of God, I could no longer express that to him in this world. It's too late now. But I still had people I could show God's love to. I committed to loving my children, family, friends, and any other neighbors that God brought to me with the help of the Holy Spirit.

15
MY OLDEST SON'S UNFORGETTABLE WORDS

In 1983 we moved from Berkeley, California, to Naperville, Illinois, where my oldest son entered junior high school. The environment in Naperville was very different from Berkeley. There were very few Asian students at the new school, whereas in California there was a large presence of Asians. He endured racism for the first time and was under stress from these experiences, both from fellow students and even from teachers. In addition, my husband gave him more pressure to perform with academic excellence. One day my son said to me, "Mom, I received a detention from my social studies teacher, so can you give me a ride back home an hour later than usual for three days?" I was so surprised to hear this from him. He had been an excellent student and was never punished when he was in school in California. I had a sense that he was being discriminated against at school.

I asked him, "What happened?" He answered, "Mom, I argued with the teacher because my grade was lower than I deserved." After the three days of detention were finished, he told me, "Mom, I think I was born with bad character." I was startled to hear my son's words. My heart hurt deeply for him because he said this after the teacher's punishment.

I responded to him, "My precious son, everyone in this world is born with a sinful nature. That is the reason why we need a Savior, Jesus Christ. However, some people don't know about it, so they aren't looking for Jesus. Yet you already discovered your sinful nature. You are a wonderful person!" His eyes began to sparkle with the hope of salvation in Jesus Christ.

As he has grown into an adult, God has blessed my oldest son both materially and spiritually. He used to work on Wall Street, and one day, his youngest brother saw a newspaper article about his promotion in the Wall Street Journal. My youngest son sent him a message of congratulations. Immediately, he sent his youngest brother a reply: "Success of this world is fleeting, success of the Spirit is foremost."

As he grew up to be a contributing member of society, there was another occasion that was deeply impressed upon me. Several years ago, he received a great promotion while switching companies. He came home from New York and said to me, "God did this for me beyond my wildest imagination." When I heard my grown-up son talking like this, I was especially happy and grateful to my heavenly Father. While he was attending elementary and junior high school, whenever he brought his excellent report cards home, we sat together, and I would ask him, "Sam, are these good grades and your smart brain from God or from yourself?" My son always answered the same way, "God gave me a good brain and grades." It is so encouraging to see that he still acknowledges that "every good and perfect gift is from above, coming down from the Father" (James 1:17).

After he married, he did not have a child for many years. He ardently waited for this new member of the family since his first day of marriage, and when his first baby, Kayla, came into the world after seven years, he was so excited. I remember seeing him holding the newborn infant in his arms and exclaiming to his younger brother, "Isn't she the most precious baby in the whole world?" He treasured her so much that I remember whenever I visited his house, he always had her in his arms, changed her diapers, and put her to sleep on top of his chest. When Kayla's first birthday arrived, all the members of the family gathered together, according to traditional Korean culture, to celebrate. This celebration of one's first birthday in Korea usually involved a big feast. The pastor graciously joined us and held a worship service for the baby's blessings. There, the pastor asked my son to pray a blessing for his baby daughter.

All of us were eager to hear what he was going to say since we had not heard him pray for many years. This would be his first time to pray publicly as a Christian, having recently returned to Christ. He began to pray, saying, "Dear Father, I have never known a love like this before. Every night when I put Kayla Grace to bed, I stare at her face, hopelessly in love." With these words, he began to cry, "Father, I do not understand Your love. You also had only one child, Jesus. And Your Son, Jesus, went to the cross and died the most painful death. On that cross, He cried out to You in utter agony, 'My God, My God, why have You forsaken Me?' If that were my daughter, Kayla, crying out to me in pain, I would have torn her off that cross and embraced her in my arms. However, You heard the cry, and though You could have saved Him, You let Him stay on that cross because of Your love for us. Father, how great can Your love be, to watch Your Son in pain and still let His sacrifice take place, all to cleanse our sins for us? I can't even begin to fathom the depths of this love." He wept as he prayed, bringing all of us to tears. We were deeply moved and amazed to hear how he felt about God's love for Jesus by comparing it to his love for his first child.

He is the atoning sacrifice for our sins, and not only for ours but also for the sins of the whole world. (1 John 2:2)

This is love: not that we loved God, but that he loved us and sent his Son as an atoning sacrifice for our sins. (1 John 4:10)

16
MY SECOND SON

One day my second son, David, who was attending Wheaton College, called me and said, "Mom, a nurse called me today telling me that our whole family needs to get a blood test as soon as possible. I'll tell you when it will be." This was startling news, so I asked him, "Why do we all have to take this test so urgently?" My son replied, "My friend and I had donated blood to the blood bank. They found that I had Hepatitis B in my blood, so they want to check if this virus runs in our family." Before we had the blood test, I was very anxious about what the results would reveal. My son David was only nineteen years old at the time. My uncle died young because of cirrhosis, which was caused by Hepatitis B. The day I heard this news, I could not sleep. I prayed to God, crying out all night, "Heavenly Father, I have lived for fifty years in this world. These years are not short, but David is only nineteen years old and has his whole life ahead of him still. So Father, please put his disease on me."

The next day my husband and I visited his dorm room and brought a healthy meal for him to eat. My husband told David about my anxiousness and weeping. My son replied, "Mom, don't worry about me. If God wants to take me to heaven, that will be really good because I could see Jesus; and if God wants me to stay here longer, it is also good because I can tell others about Jesus. Either one is great, mom, so please don't worry about me."

His words deeply moved me, and I would never forget them. When I heard what he said, I thought that his faith was much deeper than mine. He is now in his forties, and his liver has been sustained through medication. By the grace of God, he became a pastor who is excellent at preaching the gospel. The psalmist says, "I love the LORD, for he heard my voice; he heard my cry for mercy. Because he turned his ear to me, I will call on him as long as I live" (Psalm 116:1-2).

SUNJA KANG CHOI

When you were small
And just a touch away,
I covered you with blankets
Against the cool night air.
But now that you are tall
And out of reach,
I fold my hands
And cover you with prayer.

Mother's Covers by Dona Maddux Cooper[1]

17

MY FRIENDS' TRANSFORMATIONS

I had a friend who was also a member of the church I attended in Chicago, and we were also close schoolmates in Korea. When I moved to Chicago, I had a few opportunities to share my testimony with her. She listened attentively, but I did not know whether she was born again or not at that time. Years later, she told me how her life was changed. She was born again later and had a firm conviction of being saved through the blood of Jesus Christ. She was so happy, but one day she realized that she had lived as a very selfish wife. She was always thinking about receiving love from her husband. As a result, she held many complaints, anger, and frustrations in her heart.

After being born again, she found in the Bible that "it is more blessed to give than to receive" (Acts 20:35). She realized that these words encompassed both material things and spiritual things, such as unconditional love. She also read, "Love your neighbor as yourself" (Matthew 22:39), so she decided to love her husband with God's love.

First, she wanted to make him happy by treating him like her king in his daily life. Then she brought her aging in-laws from Korea to Chicago so they could take care of them. Her husband had wanted it for a long time, as he was their only son, but she selfishly did not like the idea. She began changing from a self-centered person to an others-centered person by the conviction and power of the Holy Spirit. As the Scripture says, "For we are God's workmanship, created in Christ Jesus to do good works, which God prepared in advance for us to do" (Ephesians 2:10).

I met another friend of mine when my husband was getting his doctorate at the University of California in Berkeley. She has grown to become my dearest friend. We have walked together for more than four decades. The following is her testimony in her own words.

My father was an exemplary person outside, but whenever he came home, he often raised his voice to my mother, brother, and older sister. Even though he did not swear or assault anyone, and he was rarely angry with me, I was frightened and scared whenever I heard my father's roar.

From the time I started college I lived away from home, and as soon as I graduated, I got married. It was as if I was running away to find a peaceful future. Eventually, we came to America. But after living together with my husband, I realized the terrible truth that my husband had an even hotter temper than my father. I fell into such deep despair that I couldn't express it in words. It was very difficult for me to live up to the needs of my husband. As I knew I was pregnant at that time, I decided to live for my baby.

In 1975, the year after my first son was born, I met Sunja Choi, the wife of one of my husband's classmates at the University of California in Berkeley. The first time I met her, she asked me a shocking question, "Are you sure you'll go to heaven when you die?"

I was quite surprised, but I always thought I was a good person. In fact, before marriage I had wanted to take care of orphans. In addition, I was already baptized and a devoted member in the church, and I thought of myself as incredibly patient given the difficult circumstances of my young family.

"I have confidence I will go to heaven!" I said honestly. Sunja looked surprised.

"Really? God said that there is no righteous man in the world. God, who even reads our thoughts, said that hating others is like killing them. You mean you've never hated anyone else?" she asked.

The question pierced into my heart like a fiery arrow because I thought of my husband, whom I should love the most.

That day, in the car on the way back home, I couldn't hold back my tears. The shame that I had lived with foolish values until the age of 28 and the fear of how to raise my baby well in the future made me so sad.

From the next day, I woke up at five o'clock every morning in desperation, praying for the help of the Holy Spirit, as Sunja had taught me, and began to read the Bible. Three months after reading the Word regularly, I returned to the Gospel of John after finishing the Old Testament. Strangely, my inner thoughts became exposed, as if I was standing in front of a clean mirror. I was so into the Word that the Word was reading me like an X-ray machine.

During this season, I had become so depressed that I hated meeting people, and so I decided to quit my job. Coincidentally, at that very time, UC Berkeley planned to create a new Korean language department, which was my major, so I was encouraged to help, but I turned it down on the spot. The problem of sin was the most urgent matter that I had to solve to live.

One day, as I was watching the program of a famous preacher, I heard a death row prisoner's letter of testimony. He had committed a lot of murders and was locked up in a solitary cell. He listened to a message from the preacher and received Jesus as his Savior and became a born-again Christian.

In his letter he wrote, "I am now as free as a bird in the sky, even though I will soon die." The words were so shocking to me.

Isn't he the same condemned criminal as I am? The thought suddenly popped up in my mind. I've always been guilty, and I've had a couple of abortions as well. The difference is that he was locked behind iron bars and I was locked in a cage of sin. He finally believed in God and enjoyed joy and freedom, while I did not know how to get that joy and freedom, so I was living in hell!

After thinking for a few days, I went to the Mental Clinic in Berkeley to consult about my condition because I was depressed. The psychiatrist said there was no problem. I went to another therapist, and I was told the same thing.

When my two anticipated visits were of no help, I called Mrs. Choi, who recommended that I read the Bible. With tears of despair, I said, "I used to have pride and hope that at least I was the one living a decent life, but after reading the Bible, I realized it was an illusion, and now I'm at a loss because I don't know why and how to live. I regret that I started reading the Bible."

Sunja responded with surprising joy. "That's why Jesus was crucified! We are all sinners before God. But God loved us so much that in AD 30, to restore the holy relationship, He made Jesus Christ, the Son of God, die on the cross for our sin. So don't be distressed and accept the way God has already made for you to be saved from sin."

She began to explain the gospel in more detail, starting with the Old Testament. Rudely, I slipped the phone off without listening to the rest of the story. I thought the content was so absurd that it wouldn't help me.

I wondered, How many times does someone need to be brainwashed to come to believe that Jesus, who died 2,000 years ago, could wash away their sins?

Just then, a strong impression came to my mind. "If you can understand and accept it with your understanding, it's knowledge, not faith!"

It was only then that I realized for the first time that I had no faith! I fell and prayed, literally at the end of my rope. I pleaded with God to help me find true life.

A few days later, I had a strange but vivid dream. At first, I was playing peacefully with my son on the beach, and suddenly all the surrounding people disappeared, leaving me alone in the middle of the pitch-black night, in the midst of deep water, without even a swimsuit. I was scared to death when a light appeared in the distance. I thought, *I could live if only I could get to that light,* so I swam with all my might. And when I finally made it to land, I saw the place and said with a sense of relief, "Oh, I'm alive!"

There seemed to be a holy man waiting for me. I was so glad and delighted that I ran and jumped to the door.

But why is this?

As soon as I was about to enter the house, I saw myself in the bright light that leaked through the open door, and I was naked. I couldn't go in no matter how frustrated and unfortunate I was, so I just rolled my feet and woke up.

Coincidentally, the next day I was invited to a house on condition that I would only have lunch from my husband's friend, but I met Mrs. Choi again there. When only the two of us were left there, I came to talk about the strange dream I had the day before. Her interpretation was so surprising.

"Mrs. Chung, the dark night sea points to the world darkened by human sin, and the one light shining from afar means Jesus, the light of the world. ('The people walking in darkness have seen a great light; on those living in the land of the shadow of death a light has dawned'; Isaiah 9:2)." It is God who is in the house with the light. And the fact that you didn't even have a swimsuit means you haven't yet worn the robes of salvation, which are proof that you have already been cleansed from your sins. Only when human beings stand before the presence of the Holy God can they recognize how sinful they are. At that time, it is written in the Bible that the blood of Jesus becomes a robe to hide the sin and the fault when we go out before God (Romans 13:14). But Mrs. Chung has not worn His clothes yet. Therefore, in the presence of God, the Lord of Light, the filth and shame of the heart appear to be naked. It shows a painful and disastrous spiritual state."

And she told me her testimony. While listening to the testimony, tears flowed constantly. She sought God desperately for the purpose of gaining assurance that she would go to heaven, but I was not interested in heaven nor eternity. Instead, I was looking for the solution to have a happy home in this present world. However, I felt that God was the only one who could fill my deepest needs, and I was deeply moved by Sunja's testimony.

Soon after, it dawned on me that I couldn't remember smiling for almost a year. I was always distressed and depressed without meeting people. I suddenly felt so ashamed and sorry that I couldn't bear it. But on this particular day, it seemed like something had changed. Something stirred from deep within. I fell facedown like a prisoner who had just been pardoned before the execution.

I called Him, "Lord, my Father!"

Immediately, His long-awaited love seemed to rise like a huge wave. It covered me up and became warm, breaking down my strongholds (2 Corinthians 10:4) that had been tightly closed.

How much have You loved a sinner like me; have You waited this long? I deserved to die! To save me, did You crucify Jesus, Your only Son, to bleed and die on the cross for all of my shame and pain?

What grace, what love!
How can I repay such lavish love?
Father! Now, I will dedicate the rest of my life to You.

The confession burst out of my mouth without my even realizing it as tears flowed down my cheeks. It was the moment when the purpose of my life finally changed from self-centered thoughts to the will of the Father. Since then, "God is Love" has become the logo of my email and the subject I want to shout to all the people in the world forever.

Since that spring day of 1977, my depression lifted as God's love filled my heart. I've become more joyful than ever before, so much so that the employees I work with ask me why I am always smiling. It was because I had received new life through Jesus Christ! God used my best friend Sunja to point me to Jesus, and I have walked in this new life for over forty years!

18
THE HOUSE GOD BOUGHT FOR ME

When my husband got a job transfer to a suburb of Chicago, I was so happy that we could finally buy a house with two stories and four bedrooms for the first time. This was in September of 1983. I loved this house so much. I spent time remodeling it with new paint, new tiles, new hardwood floors, and other small projects. Some of my close friends and relatives were able to visit us and stay for anywhere from a few days to a few months. I thanked God that we were able to use our house to bless and host others. Sometimes we were able to share the gospel with different guests. I also had a women's Bible study group at home. I was so delighted that I could use my house as a ministry. But after two years had passed, my husband wanted to sell the house I had grown to love. He said, "Christians should not have this sort of big house, and I am also afraid I could be laid off from work at any time." It was painful to hear these words. He quickly put our house on the market without my consent. I prayed to God that the house would not sell. God granted my petition. He would try to sell the house four times throughout the years, but every time God responded to my prayer to not have the house sold.

Eventually, in March of 2000, my husband hired a realtor whose husband was a coworker of his. She took a look around our house and then brought a couple to see the house. On the following day, the realtor came to my house with the contract papers for the sale. My husband forced me to sign my name. I couldn't argue with him in front of the realtor, but I was too angry to sign. Selling the house seemed like such an unreasonable and foolish idea both economically and for our family. Outwardly controlling my anger, I left my house and walked to a small lake in our subdivision. I cried out to God for His help as my heart trembled with anger. Tears began to fall, but God remained silent. As I eventually walked back to my house, God's Word suddenly came to me, "Wives, submit to your husbands as to the Lord. For the husband is the head of the wife as Christ is the head of the church" (Ephesians 5:22-23).

I reflected on God's Word for a while. I had been trying to keep God's words in my heart and obey them throughout my life. Since I received Jesus Christ as my Lord, the goal of my life was obeying His words. Even though I loved this house so much, I realized I had to give it up because of God's command. I had to choose either the house I loved or God's command. I concluded that I had to surrender to my husband's request. I returned home and very reluctantly signed the papers.

Soon after, we bought a smaller house, which only had three tiny bedrooms and no basement. I have four sons. The oldest son was married by that time, the second son was finishing his graduate studies on the east coast, and my two youngest were attending college nearby. Whenever summer vacation came, my youngest two sons would bring home all their belongings from their dormitories. So we ended up storing their things in the living room because there was nowhere else to put them. I was afraid that my friends would visit during that time. I missed my old house partly because we could store their things in the full-sized basement. I would even sometimes drive to our old house just to look at it.

Whenever I passed by a neighborhood like the one I had lived in before, I used to think, "My husband would never buy this kind of house again. But my oldest son is working a nice job on Wall Street. If God blesses him financially more and more, maybe my dream for a bigger house would be fulfilled through his generosity."

Four years had passed since we moved into the smaller house. I was turning sixty years old in March of 2004. My first son and his wife came from New York to celebrate my birthday. In Korean culture, the sixtieth birthday marks a special milestone. The next day, right before they departed to head back to New York, my daughter-in-law came to me and said, "Mother, Sam is going to give you a big gift when he gets a bonus next spring." The moment I heard this, I was wondering if the big gift might be a house, but I dared not ask her for a house. Instead I inquired, "What does the big gift mean?" She replied, "It's a house!" I was stunned. Oh, God! I couldn't hide my great joy in front of her. In fact, I hadn't prayed to God for a house, but God had known my deep desire and was going to grant me my dream through them as I had imagined before. My daughter-in-law suggested that I should start looking for a house even though it would be a year before the bonus came through.

In the middle of May, about two months later, one of my friends called me to stop by her house. As I drove to visit her, I saw an open house sign on the way. I passed the sign at first because I thought it was too early to look at houses. But after a few moments, I decided to return to see the house. I didn't love it, but at least it was bigger than my present house. I proceeded to visit my friend, and then came back to my house. I called my daughter-in-law and told her about the house I had seen. She said to me, "I will tell Sam about it when he comes home from work." In the evening, my son called me back and said, "Mom, we are coming to Chicago this weekend, so you should get a realtor and prepare ten more houses for us to take a look at in Naperville."

I contacted a friend of mine who was a realtor and asked for her help. She said that my son and his wife would not have enough time to take a look at them all in one weekend visit, so she suggested that we should take a look first and pick out a few homes that I was particularly interested in before they arrived. I agreed with her idea, and we looked at more than ten houses, but I couldn't find any that I loved. By the end of the day, my realtor said, "There is a house which hasn't put up a for-sale sign yet because it came on the market just a few days ago. Would you like to look at it?" I said, "Of course!"

We went to see the house. The house was very clean, well decorated, and everything seemed like it was of good quality. It was almost exactly the same size as the old house I loved. Moreover, there was a full-sized finished basement that I had always wanted. "This house is the one I want!" My son and his wife arrived early in the afternoon on Saturday. They looked at several houses and finally saw the house I liked. Our whole family agreed to buy that house.

When my son finally put in his offer, it was twenty-five thousand less than the asking price. Because of this, I couldn't sleep all night. I was really anxious about his offer. I was worried that the owner wouldn't sell the house to us at that price. As soon as morning came, I called to tell my realtor that I would pay an additional ten thousand dollars so that I wouldn't lose the house. She informed the other realtor of my new offering price. They accepted the offer.

In this way, we could finally buy this lovely house much earlier than my son had planned. I could say that all things worked out so well in His perfect time. If my son had not come to Chicago on that particular weekend, we could not have bought the house. I was certain that someone else would have bought that special house before we did, even if we had waited just one more weekend.

Shortly after, we moved into the new house. And then I saw two things I had not noticed before. There was a door inside the wall between the living room and the family room so that we could open or close it whenever we needed to. I also realized that our driveway was made of concrete instead of asphalt. I had overlooked these two things when we purchased the house. I was amazed when I took notice of these details for the first time.

At our old house, my husband and I sometimes invited many church friends over. The living room was at the right side of the front hallway and the family room was located on the other side, so one would have to cross through the kitchen to get there. We couldn't use both rooms at the same time because of the distance between them. With a big group, we always ended up crowded in one side of the house or the other. For this reason, I imagined that if I could buy another house, I would buy a house with a door between the family room and the living room so that I could open the door when needed.

As for the concrete driveway, this was also something that I had hoped for in a home. While I had been living at the old house I loved, I applied the blacktop sealant on our driveway every year by myself without anyone's help. I hired someone to do this at first, but I didn't like the way he applied the sealant, so I decided to do it on my own. Every summer, between late June and August, I would buy five large barrels of sealant for our long and wide driveway. All day long under the hot sun, I thickly spread the sealant on it. While I was working on this burdensome project, I used to dream, "If I could buy another house, I would buy a house that has a driveway made of concrete, which doesn't need blacktop sealant." Sealing and coating throughout the whole day was exhausting to me. So when I realized that our new home had a concrete driveway, I was extremely happy. I believe it was not a coincidence that God fulfilled this old dream of mine.

By the time we purchased the new house with my son, I had forgotten my desires about a convenient room layout and a concrete driveway. Finding these two features of the new house reminded me of my old wishes. I realized that only God had remembered my old dreams about the house and that He wanted me to find the exact house I had always desired. That is the reason why God brought my son here as soon as this house came on the market—to let us buy it before other people could. Actually, my son was supposed to buy me a house almost a year later because of his bonus. But instead, he bought it ten months earlier, not because of his plan but because of God's wise purposes.

At the end of this, I knelt down at my new home under the mighty and loving hand of God and prayed, "Dear wonderful Father, I obeyed Your commandment about the principles of married life four years ago. I believe that You gave me my dream house as a reward for it. I praise You for Your almighty power, wisdom, limitless grace, and love for me and the world. I will make Your amazing love known to whomever I meet. I honor You with all my heart. I love You so much! You are the greatest! You are the King of kings and the Lord of lords. I pray this in Jesus' name, amen."

We have been happily living in the house God gave me since the summer of 2004. I hope to live in this house until I go to heaven.

"For I know the plans I have for you," declares the LORD, "plans to prosper you and not to harm you, plans to give you hope and a future." (Jeremiah 29:11)

Why are you downcast, O my soul? Why so disturbed within me? Put your hope in God, for I will yet praise him, my Savior and my God. (Psalm 42:11)

19

THE GOD WHO IS ALSO FAR AWAY

It was early March of 2017, and David was going to move from his condo in Chicago to a townhouse, so I visited him on the weekend to help him move. While we were working together on a Saturday evening, he came to me and said, "Mom I want you to keep this money." What a surprise! It was $1,000. He wasn't rich, but he used to give me $100 or $200 occasionally if there was a special event. I said to him, "Wow, you are giving me a lot of money. Thank you so much! I'm really grateful and happy for this."

The next day, I returned home and prayed to God, "Dear Father, David unexpectedly gave me $1,000. I suppose this money is a bonus from You. If You want me to use it for Your will, please let me know. I really want to spend this money according to what You want. I pray this in Jesus' name, amen." After praying this, I put the money in a secret place.

One day, about two months later, I was working in the kitchen at home. A very strange thing happened to me. I found myself speaking without any self-control. "It would be better to help Zakyung instead." Three or four times, this phrase repeated itself in my voice. Speaking this was a spontaneous expression irrespective of my consciousness. Where was it coming from?

Zakyung is my older sister's youngest daughter who lives in Seoul, Korea. I was twenty-six years old when she was born, and I had not been in touch with her for a very long time, so we didn't have a close relationship. However, I am close to her oldest sister, as she is nearer in age to me. Whenever I visited Korea, I used to hear that Zakyung was living in poverty. Sometimes I would give her a small amount of money through her older sister. I didn't even know her phone number. Since I wasn't sure if this was happening from my own thoughts or from God, I ignored it.

The next day, while I was working at home as usual, I suddenly found myself saying the same words as the previous day and, again, three to four times. "It would be better to help Zakyung instead." This time I seriously wondered whether this remark came from God, so I decided to make a phone call.

I called Zakyung's sister and asked how Zakyung had been doing. She told me that Zakyung was still in a needy situation, especially with her two teenage children. I got Zakyung's phone number from her sister and immediately dialed her. She picked up the phone, and I asked her, "How have you been?" I then explained about my unusual spoken thoughts about her. After she listened to my story, she told me, "Aunt, in fact I've been praying to God for my daughter's high school entrance fee, but I am embarrassed to tell you about this matter. You don't have to help me out."

I could see that she was a very polite person and didn't want to burden me. If she knew that her heavenly Father had already prepared the money for her daughter, she wouldn't have said that. I said, "Okay, I'll send you some money." I went to the Korean-American bank in Naperville and sent her the $1,000. Later, I heard that her daughter's admission fee was $800, but I'm sure her daughter would have needed some extra money for her high school uniform and textbooks, so the $1,000 was the perfect amount for her.

After a while, Zakyung called me and said, "I told this story to the prayer members of my church." All of them were very impressed and deeply touched by her testimony, but some of them asked, "How come our God used your aunt who is living in the US rather than someone living in our country?" Because of this occurrence, I realized that South Korea is really not far away from the United States. Time and space are nothing to God.

Of course, we don't always know God's will for us; however, I have experienced that God is ruling this world in His desires and with His plan, remembering that His almighty power and knowledge are boundless and far beyond our imagination. Yes! His limitless love and grace for us are far too vast also!

"Am I only a God nearby," declares the LORD, "and not a God far away? Can anyone hide in secret places so that I cannot see him?" declares the LORD. "Do not I fill heaven and earth?" declares the LORD (Jeremiah 23:23-24)

Do not be anxious about anything, but in everything, by prayer and petition, with thanksgiving, present your requests to God. (Philippians 4:6)

20
GOD HEALED MY LIVER CANCER

My husband went to work at the prestigious Energy Institute in South Korea after his retirement in January of 2007.

While I was staying in Korea, my husband and I had a general health checkup covered by our Korean insurance policy, but neither of us had any particular symptoms of concern at that time. However, the nurses followed up with us, saying that we needed to go see both a liver and a heart specialist because of our age. We ignored her suggestion because both of us had been living in fairly good health.

It was the summer of 2008 when I began to notice that the color of my face was getting darker than ever, but I paid no serious attention to it, though I did wonder about the cause. I came back to the States in October of 2008, but I still didn't go to see a specialist to see what was wrong as life was too busy. Later, in May of 2009, I visited my youngest son, who was teaching English at a junior high school in Seoul. At that time, my digestion was getting worse and I had lost my appetite. While I was visiting him, my right leg under my knee swelled up a little sometimes.

One day, in September, I went to see a physician who was an old church friend. He ordered a blood test and an ultrasound around my abdomen. Afterward he asked me, "Hasn't your doctor in the States told you that you have cirrhosis? It resulted from your exposure to the Hepatitis B virus." It was surprising news to me. When I heard these unexpected words from the doctor, I was shocked. I hadn't even heard of the disease from any doctor I had seen so far. The only thing I had known was that one of my uncles died at a young age of cirrhosis caused by the Hepatitis B virus.

The doctor told me I had to take a CT scan, which I did a few days later. The radiologist told me that my cirrhosis had already spread to a large part of my liver. I was stunned by the news because it meant that I could be facing

73

imminent death. I brought the result of the CT to the Korean physician. He told me, "When you go back to the US, you have to see your doctor every three months for your liver checkup." That was all he talked about with me. I expected him to do some special treatments on me for my cirrhotic liver, but he didn't do anything else.

After I returned home to the States, I mostly rested because of fatigue and because I had lost my appetite. My face was getting darker than before, and I began losing weight. I went to see a doctor three months later, in March of 2010, as my doctor in Korea had advised. The physician only gave me a blood test. After the results came in, he said, "Not too bad but only one blood test isn't good. Let's take a CT in June because cirrhosis could turn into cancer later."

I returned home. I ate mostly sweet potatoes because that was all that appealed to me. I used to love all kinds of fruit, but they were no longer desirable. My body became thinner than it had ever been. Meanwhile, our alumni meeting was scheduled for early April in Chicago. I wanted to skip the meeting because of my bad health, but I couldn't miss it. It was a gathering of old students from my Korean junior high and high schools. I had been working as the treasurer for a long time, so I had to do the yearly financial report and collect dues. With reluctance, I attended the meeting. There I met the husband of an alumna who had never attended our meetings before. This was his first time in attendance. I had heard that he had been seriously ill because of his liver infection from Hepatitis B. He was hospitalized a few times about twenty years prior. But today, he seemed very healthy and energetic for a man in his seventies. I was pleased to see this.

The next day, when I was resting on the couch, a different friend who was also at the alumni meeting called me. While we were conversing, I told her about my cirrhosis even though I hadn't talked about it to any other friends yet. But there was a special reason for me to confide in her: There was a heartbreaking story about her grown-up son. When her son was twenty-nine years old, he was involved in a car accident on the highway. As a result, he was in a coma for six months. He regained consciousness but was paralyzed from his neck down and had difficulty with his eyesight. His mother used to shed tears whenever we visited them. Just as I had walked with her through her dark days, I knew that she would be a safe person to share my sorrows with. As soon as she heard me sharing about my sickness, she said, "Sunja, you should call Elder Kwon and ask him how he has been treating his liver. As you saw yesterday, he looked very healthy, but he had been seriously sick for many years."

I took her advice and called Mr. Kwon. He said, "I met a great liver specialist. He gave me a liver medication which has been working excellently. Ever since then, I feel healthier than a typical person of my age." He gave me the doctor's phone number, and I made an appointment. I brought my CT scan from Korea to the doctor. First, he ordered a blood test. After the results came in, he said to me, "You are in the final stage of cirrhosis. What I mean is that you are in the fourth stage now." I was astonished by his diagnosis and asked him, "How long do I have to live?" He replied, "Who knows?" Based on the doctor's answer, I realized that the state of my liver was critical. He gave me a prescription for liver medication and for an MRI. After I had the MRI in early June, the doctor found a cancerous tumor in my liver. He recommended that I go to a certain hospital. The doctor in the hospital asked my family whether I would have a biopsy or not. My family thought we should wait it out. About nine months later, the doctor found that the tumor had doubled in size. In June of 2011, I went in for surgery to have the tumor removed. My family surrounded me early in the morning and took turns praying for me. The specialist had warned that a small percentage of people don't make it out of the surgery. They prayed with tears for God to use the surgeons to heal me. When they were done, I asked them if I could also pray. As I prayed, I sensed God's presence in the room. I prayed, "Heavenly Father, for all my life, You have held my hand. Would You now hold my hand as I enter into surgery, and would You hold my hand throughout the surgery, and would You hold my hand out of the surgery? In Jesus' name, amen." The surgery was successful.

Afterward, the physician strongly advised me to get a liver transplant before another cancer came back. She said, "If you delay the transplant, you will no longer be a candidate for the surgery." They even called me at home a few times to move forward with the transplant. I was fearful of a liver transplant because my church friend's husband died within a year of having one because of its side effects. Also, another Korean man died one and a half years after his transplant due to different side effects.

One day, the chief nurse called me again. I told her that I needed one month before I could make a decision about it. I needed time to pray about it with my heavenly Father. I asked Him what the best treatment would be. After two weeks of praying, God gave me an idea to get a second opinion at the University of Chicago hospital. I wanted to see a liver specialist there, but I had no idea how I could get in contact. The deadline I had promised to the nurse was getting closer. My heart began to feel anxious. In the meantime, my new friend who lived in the city of Chicago called me. She asked about my health, so I told her about my current situation. Unexpectedly, she said, "Sunja, don't worry about it. My daughter is an employee at the University of Chicago. I'll ask her for someone to get in touch with." Two days later, she called me back. "Sunja, my daughter is friends with a liver specialist in the hospital!" It was such good news for me. Once again, God was providing in my need. My friend's daughter was able to get me in to see the doctor within a week, when normally it would have taken months to see this particular specialist.

I ended up meeting three doctors in one day at the University of Chicago hospitals. I brought all my medical records to them. One doctor agreed with the recommended liver transplant, but the other two doctors said that some patients like me have a greater possibility of living longer without a liver transplant. The two doctors gave me an alternative to the risky transplant that the other hospital had pressured me toward.

I got back home and prayed to God about this important matter. Afterward, I decided not to go through with the liver transplant. I had a firm conviction that my life and death belonged to God. If God wanted me to live longer, I would be able to survive without the transplant. That was in March of 2012. I continue to undergo regular MRIs and daily take the medication my new liver specialist prescribed. The result of all this is that the Hepatitis B virus in my liver is now undetectable, my appetite has slowly returned, and the darkness in my face gradually faded away.

I was hospitalized two more times when a one-centimeter cancerous tumor returned to my liver, but since the third appearance of cancer, I have been in good health. I have been cancer-free for more than five years. Sometimes I tag along with my son who is a pastor to share the gospel both stateside and overseas. I am seventy-seven years old now, but I am still keeping up with maintaining my house and working for the Kingdom of God. My life's journey is completely by God's grace.

As I reflect on this part of my journey with my liver, I recognize that God used the alumni meeting and my alumna to help bring a cure to my liver. If I had not become the treasurer of the alumni association, I would have skipped that meeting for sure. Instead, God made me the treasurer long before I got cancer. My eternal Father is the God of provision. I want to share God's words with you.

And we know that in all things God works for the good of those who love him, who have been called according to his purpose. (Romans 8:28)

I know, O LORD, that a man's life is not his own; it is not for man to direct his steps. (Jeremiah 10:23)

Though he brings grief, he will show compassion, so great is his unfailing love. (Lamentations 3:32)

21
SUPERNATURAL HEALING POWER

Stretch out your hand to heal and perform miraculous signs and wonders
through the name of your holy servant Jesus. (Acts 4:30)

Early in the spring of 1974, I heard that my friend's father, who was sixty-four years old, had a stroke that paralyzed him. He was a well-educated gentleman and a poet. His family was attending the Catholic church. He used to have a good position at a famous company. But about two years prior to his stroke, he was laid off from his job. Since then, he had tried to make a living by opening a small shop, but he failed because he had no prior business experience. In the meantime, he was working as a salesman for a bookstore. His family became so poor that he couldn't afford to go to the hospital.

When I visited him, he was resting in a small rental room with his wife. I talked about Jesus Christ and told him the story of the one lost sheep. I brought a picture of Jesus holding the one lost sheep, with the ninety-nine following behind him.

I read the story to him.

Jesus told them this parable: "Suppose one of you has a hundred
sheep and loses one of them. Does he not leave the ninety-nine in
the open country and go after the lost sheep until he finds it? And
when he finds it, he joyfully puts it on his shoulders and goes home.
Then he calls his friends and neighbors together and says, 'Rejoice
with me; I have found my lost sheep.' I tell you that in the same way
there will be more rejoicing in heaven over one sinner who repents
than over ninety-nine righteous persons who do not need to repent."
(Luke 15:3-7)

After he listened to the story, he said, "Ah! I am a lost sheep as well." His eyes began to fill with tears. I sensed that he was ready to receive Jesus Christ as his Lord and Savior. I read this verse: "We all, like sheep, have gone astray, each of us has turned to his own way; and the LORD has laid on him the iniquity of us all" (Isaiah 53:6).

I asked him, "Would you now receive Jesus Christ as your personal Savior?" He replied, "Yes," and then he prayed to God.

> Dear God, I feel I am just like Your lost sheep. I have gone astray
> from Your presence for a long time. But now I want to turn back to
> You. Please accept me as Your returning sheep. I pray this in Jesus'
> name, amen.

While I was listening to his earnest prayer, great joy flowed into my heart. So I told him, "Let's pray to our almighty Father for your healing." I placed my right hand on his paralyzed right leg and began to pray. As my prayer continued, something incredible began to take place. I felt a supernatural power traveling from my heart through my right arm into his right leg. I was so stunned by the incredible power because I had never experienced anything like it. After the prayer, I wondered if something significant took place, but I was afraid that he couldn't stand up even though I wanted to say to him, "Stand up, please." I sat in silence contemplating what to say when he said, "I feel like standing up." He tried to stand up and slowly started to walk leaning against the wall. His wife was so surprised and said to me that he couldn't move at all before! By God's great mercy and compassion, he was healed by his faith in Christ. All of us in the room rejoiced to see him and began to praise the Lord! His faith had healed him through the power of the Holy Spirit in me. About four months later, I came to the US to reunite with my husband, who was studying in Austin. Months later, I received a letter from the healed man with a drawing of the cross he had made:

In his letter, he still had great joy from meeting his Creator and from receiving eternal life. He also said, "I am so happy that I could meet you, as if I met an angel of God." However, very sadly, he had a second stroke about two years later and passed away. I look forward to the day when I will see him again by the river of living water in the Kingdom of God.

As Jesus was on his way, the crowds almost crushed him. And a woman was there who had been subject to bleeding for twelve years, but no one could heal her. She came up behind him and touched the edge of his cloak, and immediately her bleeding stopped.

"Who touched me?" Jesus asked.

When they all denied it, Peter said, "Master, the people are crowding and pressing against you."

But Jesus said, "Someone touched me; I know that power has gone out from me."

Then the woman, seeing that she could not go unnoticed, came trembling and fell at his feet. In the presence of all the people, she told why she had touched him and how she had been instantly healed. Then he said to her, "Daughter, your faith has healed you. Go in peace."

(Luke 8:42-48)

22

THE SPIRIT OF UNDERSTANDING
AND KNOWLEDGE

The Spirit of the LORD will rest on him—the Spirit of wisdom and of understanding, the Spirit of counsel and of power, the Spirit of knowledge and of the fear of the LORD. (Isaiah 11:2)

As I shared before, since the Holy Spirit rested on me, the words of the Bible became clearly understandable and real to me. But there were other amazing things that happened as well. I would like to share one of them with you.

I was scheduled to give students a lecture on fashion design at a university. I had to prepare for a course on the subject by the end of February before the spring semester began in 1969. In 1968, there were no textbooks in this field for college students in South Korea. Therefore, I had to translate either books on fashion design from the US or from Japan. I already knew English, but I needed to learn Japanese. I decided to go to the Academy to learn Japanese. I studied there for three months. Then I tried to translate the Japanese college textbook that I had bought. However, it was too hard for me to understand. Although I worked hard on it, I still couldn't understand much of it. At the same time that I was struggling with this difficult situation, my spiritual journey had just begun, so all of my efforts for the book were temporarily put on hold. A week after I was born again of the Holy Spirit, I was reminded of my lecture one day. It was ten days before March, and there was not much time left. So I opened the Japanese textbook with a feeling of anxiety. To my surprise, I could now understand all the contents easily. The book was so different now. In this way, I experienced God's miraculous power in an intellectual area as well as a spiritual area.

Five years later, I was able to write my own college textbook entitled *Fashion Design*. It was the first of its kind published in Korean, all by the grace of God. The book was published in 1974, shortly before I came to the United States.

23
MY FRIEND'S WONDROUS DREAM

In May of 1979, after my husband got his PhD, we started a Bible study group with Korean foreign students in the Berkeley and Oakland area. One student's wife didn't attend even though I invited her several times. One day she showed up to our group for the first time and shared with us the reason why she came that day. The night before she came, she had a dream. In her dream, she was in a large hall. There were many people inside the hall, and there was a choir that was singing beautiful hymns in a corner. At that moment, the sky suddenly opened, and she saw a man who was holding the Bible in one hand coming down from the sky into the hall. He stood in the hall and said to the crowd, "I will pick up one person among you and show this person heaven." She was picked up by the angel. He held her in his one arm, and they flew up together into the sky.

After a while, she stood in heaven, which looked like a holy castle. There were many white mansions as pure as a baby lamb. The surroundings of heaven were calm, holy, and peaceful. While she was looking around, a dignified voice said, "You saw heaven. Now go down and tell them what you have seen." Right after that voice, she fell downward back into the same hall she had been in before. Swarms of people came around her and asked, "You were here a little while ago. Where have you been?" Then she woke up from the dream. It was about four o'clock in the morning. She told the story to her husband, who also was not a Christian. After hearing her share about the dream, he replied, "You had better go to church." She concluded the story by telling us that this was the reason why she came to the Bible study that day. Afterward, her whole family became sincere Christians.

I saw the Holy City, the new Jerusalem, coming down out of heaven from God, prepared as a bride beautifully dressed for her husband. (Revelation 21:2)

In my Father's house are many rooms. . . . I am going there to prepare a place for you. And if I go and prepare a place for you, I will come back and take you to be with me that you also may be where I am. (John 14:2-3)

EPILOGUE
HOW TO BE BORN AGAIN:
THE POWER OF THE BLOOD OF JESUS CHRIST

The blood will be a sign for you on the houses where you are; and when I
see the blood, **I will pass over you**. No destructive plague will touch you
when I strike Egypt. (Exodus 12:13)

Before Jesus came to this world, God gave instructions to the Israelites on
how they could be saved during the Passover. Passover is still the oldest and
most important religious festival in Israel, commemorating God's deliverance
of the Israelites from slavery in Egypt and His creation of the nation of Israel.

Get rid of the old yeast that you may be a new batch without yeast—
as you really are. For Christ, our Passover lamb, has been sacrificed.
(1 Corinthians 5:7)

The Power of the Blood of Jesus Christ

As we live in this world, we are always in need of different kinds of soaps and
detergents to cleanse our clothes and our bodies, including some dirty spots,
stains, and the things around us. Well, have you ever thought about the
cleansing of your inmost conscience or heart? Through the Creator's Word,
the Bible, we can discover the answer to this question.

Around 700 BC, God's prophet Isaiah prophesied these words from God:

Wash and make yourselves clean. Take your evil deeds out of my
sight! Stop doing wrong. . . . Come now, let us reason together," says
the LORD. "Though your sins are like scarlet, they shall be as white
as snow; though they are red as crimson, they shall be like wool.
(Isaiah 1:16, 18)

I have swept away your offenses like a cloud, your sins like the morning mist. (Isaiah 44:22)

I, even I, am he who blots out your transgressions, for my own sake, and remembers your sins no more. (Isaiah 43:25)

And through the prophet Zechariah, God said "On that day a fountain will be opened to the house of David and the inhabitants of Jerusalem, to cleanse them from sin and impurity" (Zechariah 13:1).

Through these passages, God is clearly saying that our inner sins and impurities shall be washed as white as snow. Isn't this good news? And what cleanser has God provided for our sanctification?

Before searching for the answer to this question, we need to see how God looks at mankind's mentality and the condition of our hearts. God says through the prophet Jeremiah: "The heart is deceitful above all things and beyond cure. Who can understand it? I the LORD search the heart and examine the mind" (Jeremiah 17:9-10); and in Isaiah: "Their words and deeds are against the LORD, defying his glorious presence" (Isaiah 3:8). God also speaks through numerous passages in the New Testament regarding mankind's condition:

As for you, you were dead in your transgressions and sins, in which you used to live when you followed the ways of this world and of the ruler of the kingdom of the air, the spirit who is now at work in those who are disobedient. All of us also lived among them at one time, gratifying the cravings of our sinful nature and following its desires and thoughts. Like the rest, we were by nature objects of wrath. (Ephesians 2:1-3)

For since the creation of the world God's invisible qualities—his eternal power and divine nature—have been clearly seen, being understood from what has been made, so that men are without excuse. For although they knew God, they neither glorified him as God nor gave thanks to him, but their thinking became futile and their foolish hearts were darkened. (Romans 1:20-21)

Furthermore, since they did not think it worthwhile to retain the knowledge of God, he gave them over to a depraved mind, to do what ought not to be done. They have become filled with every kind of wickedness, evil, greed and depravity. They are full of envy, murder, strife, deceit and malice. They are gossips, slanderers, God-haters, insolent, arrogant and boastful; they invent ways of doing evil; they disobey their parents; they are senseless, faithless, heartless, ruthless. Although they know God's righteous decree that those who do such things deserve death, they not only continue to do these very things but also approve of those who practice them. (Romans 1:28-32)

Before ascending to heaven, Jesus said that the Holy Spirit would come and prove the world wrong "in regard to sin, because men do not believe in me" (John 16:9). Furthermore, these other New Testament passages also talk about sin:

We accept man's testimony, but God's testimony is greater because it is the testimony of God, which he has given about his Son. Anyone who believes in the Son of God has this testimony in his heart. Anyone who does not believe God has made him out to be a liar, because he has not believed the testimony God has given about his Son. (1 John 5:9-10)

For all have sinned and fall short of the glory of God. (Romans 3:23)

As it is written: "There is no one righteous, not even one." (Romans 3:10)

For the wages of sin is death. (Romans 6:23)

Therefore, just as sin entered the world through one man, and death through sin, and in this way death came to all men, because all sinned. (Romans 5:12)

Just as man is destined to die once, and after that to face judgment. (Hebrews 9:27)

Is there any hope for us to be freed from God's judgment and the penalty of death, which is the consequence of sin? This is God's reply in the second half of Romans 6:23: "For the wages of sin is death, but the gift of God is eternal life in Christ Jesus our Lord." The apostle Paul also writes:

But God demonstrates his own love for us in this: While we were still sinners, Christ died for us. Since we have now been justified by his blood, how much more shall we be saved from God's wrath through him! (Romans 5:8-9)

We also see this in the book of Revelation, as John says this about Jesus Christ: "To him who loves us and has freed us from our sins by his blood"

(Revelation 1:5). The power of the blood of Jesus Christ can also be seen in 1 John 1:7: "The blood of Jesus, his Son, purifies us from all sin."

In these passages from God's Word, we learn that the blood of Jesus Christ is the only answer that liberates us from the wrath of God's judgment. Our sovereign Creator tells us that the blood of His only Son is the perfect cleanser for our filthy hearts. Now let's move on to the reason why we must believe in Jesus Christ and His blood to be a righteous person in the sight of a Holy God.

First, we have to grasp why Jesus Christ, when He was a young man at the age of thirty-three, shed His precious blood on the cross. We also have to understand that Jesus Christ Himself is the only way to God. Jesus said, "I am the way and the truth and the life. No one comes to the Father except through me" (John 14:6). The apostle Peter wrote, "Christ died for sins once for all, the righteous for the unrighteous, to bring you to God" (1 Peter 3:18). Just as there are many laws to govern the nations on earth, so there are many laws through which God governs the world, both physically and spiritually. What are these laws? Here is God's Word on the law of atonement, so be alert!

"For the life of a creature is in the blood, and I have given it to you to make atonement for yourselves on the altar; *it is the blood that makes atonement for one's life*" (Leviticus 17:11) and "*In fact, the law requires that nearly everything be cleansed with blood*, and without the shedding of blood there is no forgiveness" (Hebrews 9:22). God, through His law, spoke about the essence and function of blood, in that there is no forgiveness of sin without the shedding of blood. Therefore, what kind of blood is needed to pardon our sin? To see more clearly regarding this blood that atones for sin, let us go back to the book of Exodus in the Old Testament, written around 1450 BC by God's wonderful servant Moses.

The Blood of the Passover Lamb

The story of the Lord's Passover, which occurred in Egypt during the exodus of the Israelites, is the most meaningful and awesome event in the history of Israel. Around 1580 BC, Pharaoh, the king of Egypt, started to take advantage of the Hebrews as their slaves. He put slave masters over the Hebrews to oppress them with harsh labor. The Hebrews built two cities, Pithom and Rameses, for Pharaoh in Egypt. The Hebrews also lived in misery due to hard labor in laying brick and mortar as well as other intense work in the fields, and so the Egyptians treated the Hebrews ruthlessly for approximately 130 years.

The Israelites groaned deeply in agony from their slavery. Their cry for help went up to God and He heard them, and He was very much concerned for their suffering. So God decided to rescue His people from the hand of the Egyptians and to bring them into a good and spacious land, a land flowing with milk and honey that God had promised to their forefathers. (This Promised Land also points to the eternal homeland of Christians.) Then God called to Moses from within a burning bush and said,

> The cry of the Israelites has reached me, and I have seen the way the Egyptians are oppressing them. So now, go. I am sending you to Pharaoh to bring my people the Israelites out of Egypt. . . . I will be with you. (Exodus 3:9-10, 12)

And God gave Moses a staff with which to perform the miraculous and wondrous signs of God. But Pharaoh did not relent after nine of the wondrous signs were performed among the Egyptians. But for now, let's give our attention to the tenth and last sign: Every Egyptian firstborn male, both humans and animals, would be killed. However, God distinguished between the Egyptians and the Israelites. And what was this distinction? God commanded Moses to do this:

> Tell the whole community of Israel that on the tenth day of this month each man is to take a lamb for his family, one for each household. . . . The animals you choose must be year-old males without defect, and you may take them from the sheep or the goats. Take care of them until the fourteenth day of the month, when all the people of the community of Israel must slaughter them at twilight. Then they are to take some of the blood and put it on the sides and tops of the doorframes of the houses where they eat the lambs. (Exodus 12:3, 5-7)

Furthermore, and these are very important words:

> The blood will be a sign for you on the houses where you are; *and when I see the blood, I will pass over you.* No destructive plague will touch you when I strike Egypt. This is a day you are to commemorate; for the generations to come you shall celebrate it as a festival to the LORD—a lasting ordinance. (Exodus 12:13-14)

Since that special night, the Passover feast has been celebrated by the Jews for generations. They commemorate God's deliverance of the Israelites from slavery and protection from the death of their firstborn in the land of Egypt.

Through all these wondrous occurrences and plagues, some may have wondered why God instructed the Israelites to keep only the Passover as a lasting ordinance but not the other nine plagues. An important detail of the first Passover in Egypt was that one-year-old male lambs without defect were killed in order to spare the firstborn sons of the Israelites. The importance of this detail can be seen in the New Testament, which starts about 1,500 years later, when John the Baptist, full of the Holy Spirit, proclaimed that Jesus Christ was the Lamb of God. In John 1:29, he said, "Look, the Lamb of God, who takes away the sin of the world!" Furthermore, the apostle Paul wrote, "For Christ, our Passover lamb, has been sacrificed" (1 Corinthians 5:7). And the apostle Peter said that we were not redeemed with gold or silver "but with the precious blood of Christ, a lamb without blemish or defect" (1 Peter 1:19).

Why would these three men of God say that Jesus Christ is the "Lamb of God?" And specifically, for Paul to say that He is our Passover lamb. What is the connection between Jesus Christ and the lamb from Passover? To answer this question, we must look at the death of Jesus Christ in the New Testament, around AD 30.

Jesus said to His disciples, "As you know, the Passover is two days away—and the Son of Man will be handed over to be crucified" (Matthew 26:2). Jesus then instructed His disciples Peter and John: "Go and make preparations for us to eat the Passover" (Luke 22:8). So the disciples did as Jesus directed and prepared the Passover. And while they were eating, Jesus took the bread, gave thanks, broke it, and gave it to His disciples, saying, "Take and eat; this is my body" (Matthew 26:26). Jesus then took the cup, gave thanks, and offered it to His disciples, saying, "Drink from it, all of you. This is my blood of the covenant, which is poured out for many for the forgiveness of sin" (Matthew 26:27-28.) We then learn that the next day, after Jesus had been arrested, "Early in the morning, all the chief priests and the elders of the people came to the decision to put Jesus to death" (Matthew 27:1).

As the day continued, we see the following take place:

Meanwhile Jesus stood before the governor. . . .

Now it was the governor's custom at the Feast to release a prisoner chosen by the crowd. At that time they had a notorious prisoner, called Barabbas. So when the crowd had gathered, Pilate asked them, "Which one do you want me to release to you: Barabbas, or Jesus who is called Christ?" . . .

But the chief priests and the elders persuaded the crowd to ask for Barabbas and to have Jesus executed.

"Which of the two do you want me to release to you?" asked the governor.

"Barabbas," they answered.

"What shall I do, then, with Jesus who is called Christ?" Pilate asked.

They all answered, "Crucify him!"

"Why? What crime has he committed?" asked Pilate.

But they shouted all the louder, "Crucify him!" . . .

Then he released Barabbas to them. But he had Jesus flogged, and handed him over to be crucified." (Matthew 27:11, 15-17, 20-23, 26)

We then see in John's Gospel:

So the soldiers took charge of Jesus. Carrying his own cross, he went out to the place of the Skull (which in Aramaic is called Golgotha). Here they crucified him, and with him two others—one on each side and Jesus in the middle. . . . Later, knowing that all was now completed, and so that the Scripture would be fulfilled, Jesus said, "I am thirsty." A jar of wine vinegar was there, so they soaked a sponge in it, put the sponge on a stalk of the hyssop plant, and lifted it to Jesus' lips. When he had received the drink, Jesus said, "It is finished." With that, he bowed his head and gave up his spirit. (John 19:16-18, 28-30)

So in this way, the Jews killed Jesus, who was innocent as well as being the Son of God who is holy, in place of the criminal Barabbas, who had a sinful nature just the same as the rest of humanity. God permitted this to happen so that Jesus, His only Son, would be like the sacrificial lamb of the Passover for humans. It was on the day of preparation when the lambs of the first Passover had been killed. About 1,500 years later, the Lamb of God, who was without defect, was killed on Calvary to provide the blood of redemption not only for Jews but also for the whole world. The apostle John wrote this about Jesus: "He is the atoning sacrifice for our sins, and not only for ours but also for the sins of the whole world" (1 John 2:2).

In approximately AD 30, the greatest historical and spiritual event happened in the land of Judea, according to the longtime plan of the Creator, in order to cleanse our blemished hearts. And as such, God finally saved all humankind from the power of sin and death, just as God saved the Israelites from the attacking Egyptian army when they passed through the Red Sea. In other words, as the ancient Israelites needed the blood of lambs to escape and avoid the death of their firstborn sons, so we need the blood of Jesus Christ to escape and avoid God's final judgment of wrath. Jesus said, "I give them eternal life, and they shall never perish; no one can snatch them out of my hand" (John 10:28). Likewise, Jesus says, "Whoever believes in the Son has eternal life, but whoever rejects the Son will not see life, for God's wrath remains on him" (John 3:36). And just before Jesus gave up His breath, He said, "It is finished" (John 19:30). And what was it that was finished through Jesus' death? The answer is written in Scripture!

"Then he said, 'Here I am, I have come to do your will.' He sets aside the first to establish the second. And by that will, we have been made holy through the sacrifice of the body of Jesus Christ once for all" (Hebrews 10:9-10). And Jesus says, "My food . . . is to do the will of him who sent me and to finish his work" (John 4:34).

Our Savior, Jesus Christ, finished His Father's will through His sacrificial death. That is, Jesus purchased and redeemed men and women for God from every tribe and nation with His blood. Therefore, God is saying to us now, "Just as I had passed over the houses where I could see the blood of the lamb on the doorways in Egypt so that no destructive plague would touch the Israelites, so I will pass over men's sin whenever I see the blood of my son Jesus on the doorways of their hearts." Jesus said, "Here I am! I stand at the door and knock. If anyone hears my voice and opens the door, I will come in and eat with him, and he with me" (Revelation 3:20). The way of salvation made by the blood of Jesus Christ is God's *new* covenant. Therefore, the blood of the lamb, which saved the Israelites' firstborn sons, was a foreshadowing of the blood of God's eternal Lamb, Jesus, who saves the whole world from their sin.

Since the first Passover, the Israelites have killed countless animals, especially pure little lambs, year after year as a sin offering for the atonement of the Israelites. But we no longer need to offer sacrifices because Jesus Christ Himself became our eternal sacrificial offering to atone for our sins through God's new covenant. We read in Hebrews: "The time is coming, declares the Lord, when I will make a new covenant with the house of Israel and with the house of Judah. It will not be like the covenant I made with their forefathers when I took them by the hand to lead them out of Egypt" (Hebrews 8:8-9). And Hebrews later explains: "In calling this covenant 'new,' he has made the first one obsolete; and what is obsolete and aging will soon disappear" (Hebrews 8:13). Furthermore, the apostle Paul wrote, "Get rid of the old yeast that you may be a new batch without yeast—as you really are. For Christ, our Passover lamb, has been sacrificed" (1 Corinthians 5:7).

Through these Scriptures, we realize that we are no longer living in the old covenant but in the new covenant. As I have said before, the Old Testament's lambs were only a symbol of Jesus Christ. Therefore, God's old law of atonement was only a temporary one until the new law came through the blood of Jesus. It is also the reason why the Bible is divided into the Old Testament and the New Testament. The old covenant is no longer effective for the forgiveness of our sin. Instead, God's only Son purifies us from our sin, without any cost or any righteous achievements on our part, but only through our faith in Jesus. Indeed, the heart of the New Testament is the death and resurrection of Jesus Christ for man's eternal salvation.

Therefore, our Lord's longing is that our lives may be divided much as history is labeling dates: AD, meaning *Anno Domini*, or in the year of our Lord, and prior to that, BC, meaning "Before Christ." Jesus said, "For my

Father's will is that everyone who looks to the Son and believes in him shall have eternal life, and I will raise him up at the last day" (John 6:40). And He also said, "For God did not send his Son into the world to condemn the world, but to save the world through him" (John 3:17). We also see this exchange between Jesus and His disciples: "Then they asked him, 'What must we do to do the works God requires?' Jesus answered, 'The work of God is this: to believe in the one he has sent'" (John 6:28-29).

Dear precious friends, about 3,500 years ago, God ordered that "the people of the community of Israel must slaughter them [the lambs] at twilight" (Exodus 12:6). About 1,500 years after that, God sent His Son to Israel as the Lamb of redemption in the twilight of the era. Since Jesus Christ went up to heaven after fulfilling God's new covenant, our earthly time has been running on toward midnight, and I believe that midnight grows darker and will soon bring the dawn of the new age.

Jesus said this before His sacrifice for us:

Do not let your hearts be troubled. Trust in God; trust also in me. In my Father's house are many rooms; if it were not so, I would have told you. I am going there to prepare a place for you. And if I go and prepare a place for you, I will come back and take you to be with me that you also may be where I am. (John 14:1-3)

Our Savior Jesus Christ will return to take us home when He has finished preparing our dwelling place in heaven. Jesus Christ said to His disciple John around AD 95 on the island of Patmos near modern-day Turkey, "Behold, I am coming soon! My reward is with me, and I will give to everyone according to what he has done. I am the Alpha and the Omega, the First and the Last, the Beginning and the End" (Revelation 22:12-13). When Jesus returns from heaven with the glory of the King of kings, we will see a new heaven and a new earth, just as He promised. The first heaven and the first earth will pass away, and there will no longer be any sea.

Dear precious friends: Are you ready to say, "Come, Lord Jesus Christ"? Have you washed your heart with the blood of Jesus Christ? As you know, our salvation comes from our one and only Savior and His pure blood. The apostle John wrote, "Blessed are those who wash their robes, that they may have the right to the tree of life and may go through the gates into the city" (Revelation 22:14). And the apostle Peter said:

The day of the Lord will come like a thief. The heavens will disappear with a roar; the elements will be destroyed by fire, and the earth and everything in it will be laid bare. Since everything will be destroyed in this way, what kind of people ought you to be? You ought to live holy and godly lives. . . . But in keeping with his promise, we are looking forward to a new heaven and a new earth, the home of righteousness. (2 Peter 3:10-11, 13)

Now, no one knows how much time we have. So before we depart this earth, we should make up our minds on where we will spend our eternity: heaven or hell. Our merciful, eternal Father has been longing for His lost children to return to Him. *If any of you wants to meet God, please ask Him. The Spirit of the Lord will come to you to direct you in the way you should go.* "But when he, the Spirit of truth, comes, he will guide you into all the truth" (John 16:13). *Without the power of the Holy Spirit, no one can believe in Jesus Christ, God, or His spiritual world. So because of that, please ask God to help you obtain the citizenship of heaven,* our eternal homeland. God reminds us of this truth through the apostle Paul: "If you confess with your mouth, 'Jesus is Lord,' and believe in your heart that God raised him from the dead, you will be saved" (Romans 10:9). Would you sing the words of the hymn "I Hear Thy Welcome Voice" together with me?

I hear Thy welcome voice
That calls me, Lord, to Thee,
For cleansing in Thy precious blood
That flowed on Calvary.

I am coming, Lord!
Coming now to Thee!
Wash me, cleanse me in the blood
That flowed on Calvary!

Tho' coming weak and vile,
Thou dost my strength assure;
Thou dost my vileness fully cleanse,
Till spotless all, and pure.[1]

I saw the Holy City, the new Jerusalem, coming down out of heaven from God, prepared as a bride beautifully dressed for her husband. And I heard a loud voice from the throne saying, "Now the dwelling of God is with men, and he will live with them. They will be his people, and God himself will be with them and be their God. He will wipe every tear from their eyes. There will be no more death or mourning or crying or pain, for the old order of things has passed away."

He who was seated on the throne said, "I am making everything new!" Then he said, "Write this down, for these words are trustworthy and true."

He said to me: "It is done. I am the Alpha and the Omega, the Beginning and the End. To him who is thirsty I will give to drink without cost from the spring of the water of life. He who overcomes will inherit all this, and I will be his God and he will be my son. But the cowardly, the unbelieving, the vile, the murderers, the sexually immoral, those who practice magic arts, the idolaters and all liars—their place will be in the fiery lake of burning sulfur. This is the second death." (Revelation 21:2-8)

He has made everything beautiful in its time. He has also set eternity in the hearts of men; Yet they cannot fathom what God has done from beginning to end.

Ecclesiastes 3:11

ABOUT THE AUTHOR

Sunja Kang Choi has lived a full and abundant life walking with her Lord and Savior, Jesus Christ. She was born in a small town and raised in Daegu, the third largest city in Korea, where her father would become the mayor. Sunja was one of eight children in her family. She graduated from Kyungbook National University in 1966 and received a graduate degree in 1968. Her university immediately hired her to become a Teacher's Assistant from 1968–1970 before becoming a Full Instructor in the Department of Home Economics, where she worked from 1970–1974. While there, she wrote a college textbook on fashion design that was published in Korea in 1975.

Sunja sacrificially came to the United States in 1974 to support her husband, Stephen Ung So Choi, in pursuing his masters degree at the University of Texas, Austin, and his PhD at the University of California, Berkeley. Stephen would go on to become a pioneer in the nascent field of nanofluids. Sunja never returned to academia but focused her attention on her four boys: Samuel, David, John, and Paul. More importantly, she poured herself into witnessing for Christ and helping lead people into God's Kingdom. She has directly or indirectly brought thousands of lives to Christ. At Berkeley, she started a women's Bible study whose members have become a diaspora of witnesses for Christ all over Asia and the US. In Illinois, she witnessed to those who were in need not only at churches but also in the aisles of supermarkets or wherever she could meet people! Sunja's love for Christ is infectious, and her daily walk radiantly reflects Christ's love, joy, and peace. A shorter version of her testimony was published in Korea in a book of twelve testimonies. The title roughly translates to English as *Joyful People Who Put Their Faith in Christ*. Her testimony was also published in a Korean Christian magazine called *New Home*. As Sunja wrote her testimony, she felt her heart deeply warmed by the Holy Spirit. She is hoping and praying that you would also encounter the intimate presence of the Holy Spirit as you read this book.

LETTERS FROM SUNJA'S SONS
ON HER 70TH BIRTHDAY

From Sunung

I recall the black-and-white pictures of you carrying me on your back (Uh-Boo-Bah) in Korea. You look so young and beautiful with so much hope in your eyes. You were a professor in Korea, but you gave that all up to put your husband and children first in a foreign land. It must have been difficult to live in a country without knowing the language and with your friends and family thousands of miles away, but you never took that anxiety out on us. You were always so loving and kind. You grew up in a beautiful home in Korea, the daughter of the mayor, but when you came to America, we lived like poor people. I don't remember you ever complaining. Instead, you made what we had into a happy home. You went to garage sales to get our furniture and clothes, you humbled yourself to that degree. When we were disciplined by Abba, you always came to our room later to comfort us. You have shown us with your actions the true love that Jesus gives His children. My only complaint is that you made me play the piano. ☺

Now, as I reflect on the love you poured out on us, I know that I haven't given you back nearly enough. That hope in your eyes in the old pictures, I would think, was the hope that your children would grow up healthy and strong (it is the only thing that I ask God for my own children). I hope we have made you proud of us and that your sacrifice you made for your children was worth it, and I promise to give you back more and more through the next few years.

Happy birthday, Umma!

Love, Sunung

From David

Dearest Mom,

I hope that this scrapbook honors you and shows you a small glimpse into the impact you have made around the world. These letters came from as far as China and Latvia and as close as Naperville. Most importantly, they come to you from your four sons who you helped raise to become men of God.

My words feel inadequate to describe to you the gratitude I feel for your life. I remember as a kid crying when I saw the hurt you received time and time again. I remember when I gave you all my money (about five dollars 😊) because I thought you would need it more than me. I remember how you would serve us three delicious meals, wash the dishes, do our laundry, have a snack ready when we came home from school, and give us rides to play sports and piano and school events.

You have exceeded the model woman from Proverbs 31 with your hard work, devotion to your family, and love for the Lord. How many memories I have of seeing you glorify Jesus with your life! As a little kid in Berkeley, I would wake up to see the coffee table surrounded by women who were learning the Bible from you and coming to know Jesus for the first time. In Chicago, I would see you invite people from church to our home that no one else wanted to be with, but you loved them with God's love. When we went to Asia, you shared Christ with people from so many different backgrounds. We have shared so many times studying God's Word together and praying on our knees.

Mom, when I saw you crying at the doctor's when they discovered a tumor in your liver, my heart sank. I wept as I prayed with you that day because I could not imagine a life without you. I had to wrestle with God that week about how much I believed in heaven. I wanted to know deep in my heart that when God takes you from this world in His perfect time you would truly be happy and loved forever. I needed to know that when I leave this world, I will be reunited with you forever, in the presence of the One you have taught your four sons to love most: Jesus. Thank you for modeling to us what a woman of God looks like up close. Thank you for loving us even when we were mean to you and were undeserving.

You always smile like a little girl when you tell me, "I am a princess. I am a daughter of the King!" Because of you and your example, your four sons can smile too, because we are now princes, sons of the King!

With deepest love,
Your son David

From Johan
To my most favorite Umma in the world,
If growing up with Abba as our dad was so difficult and tough for us, I always wondered how much more difficult and tough it must have been for you to endure many more years of being his wife. Umma, you were the cool wind to Abba's scorching heat. You were the grace that balanced Abba's "justice." You were the gentleness that tempered Abba's harshness. You were the reason all of your sons turned out okay.

I believe that for persevering through over 40 years of marriage to Abba, God has rewarded you as a mom with four sons who will fight for you, who desire only good for you (to make up for all the painful years), and who want to give back to you as much as you've so sacrificially and lovingly given to us, knowing that there's no way we could ever repay you.

Your recent health issues have highlighted the fact that our time with you is short. I will do whatever I can in my limited power to make sure these last several years will be your best several years. I thank God He provided the best mom a son could ever ask for in you. Thanks for being there. Thanks for showing Jesus' love through your love. Thanks for the thousands of meals. Thanks for cutting up the tens of thousands of fruit and making tens of thousands of cups of tea for us. Thanks for the thousands of loads of laundry you washed, dried, and folded. Thanks for attending my piano recitals and cello concerts when Abba wouldn't. Thanks for letting me watch Sesame Street when Abba wouldn't let me. Thanks for showing all of us how to truly love and take care of another human being, even when he/she does not deserve it.

I love you, Umma. Happy birthday!

Johan

From Paul

Umma,

I love you so much. Words can never express what you have meant to me and this family who you have poured out your beautiful life for. The older you get, the more I see how many imperfections I have, the more I realize how much your love has been a saving and redeeming blanket in my life. And ultimately, it reminds me how much I need Jesus and that God is with me even in my darkest moments. How can I thank you enough for that?

Umma, I pray for only the best in your life, and I hope we boys bring you some measure of joy for all the anguish we caused growing up. Thank you for loving me despite how bad I can be. You taught me Jesus.

Love so much,

Paul

NOTES

3 SEARCHING AFTER GOD
1. Charles Wesley, "Unwearied Earnestness," verse 1 (1741).
2. Edward Hopper, "Jesus, Savior, Pilot Me," verse 1 (1871).

4 GOD'S MESSAGE TO ME
1. John Newton, "Amazing Grace! (How Sweet the Sound)," verse 1 (1779).
2. Fanny Crosby, "Blessed Assurance," verse 1 (1820–1915).
3. Eliza E. Hewitt, "Jesus Has Lifted the Load," verse 1 and refrain (1956).

17 MY SECOND SON
1. Quoted in "The Unlocked Door," from *Chicken Soup for the Mother's Soul: Stories to Open the Hearts and Rekindle the Spirits of Mothers* (Originally published: Deerfield Beach, FL: Health Communications, 1997).

EPILOGUE
1. Lewis Hartsough, "I Hear Thy Welcome Voice," verses 1 and 2, refrain (1872).

Made in the USA
Coppell, TX
19 April 2022

76748973R10069